No More Excuses!

No More Excuses!

The Five Accountabilities for Personal and Organizational Growth

SAM SILVERSTEIN

Sound Wisdom
P.O. Box 310
Shippensburg, PA 17257-0310

Previously Published ISBN 13: 978-0470531921

For more information on foreign distribution, call 717-530-2122.
Reach us on the Internet: www.soundwisdom.com

ISBN 13 TP: 978-0-7684-0752-5
ISBN 13 Ebook: 978-0-7684-0753-2

For Worldwide Distribution, Printed in the U.S.A.

3 4 5 6 7 8 / 18 17 16 15

For Renee, Geoffrey, Sara, Jaclyn, and Allison. You inspire, challenge, and support me, and for that I am eternally grateful.

CONTENTS

Contents

ACKNOWLEDGMENTS

I would like to thank the following:

My many friends and colleagues who helped me to arrange interviews with the accountability masters.

The more than 50 accountability masters from around the world who contributed their thoughts and ideas and helped me add meaning and impact to this project.

INTRODUCTION: YOUR COMPETITIVE ADVANTAGE

S ome people achieve extraordinary things in life; others do not. The difference between the two groups lies in accountability.

True story: Early in the Minnesota Twins 2009 exhibition season, Twins manager Ron Gardenhire discovered a note on his desk from Justin Morneau, his star first baseman. It read: "Gardy: I forgot to run sprints after the workouts yesterday; I am fining myself." Next to the note was a hundred-dollar bill.

Was Justin Morneau accountable because he was a superstar, or was he a superstar because he was accountable?

No More Excuses is a way of looking at the world—a standard to which we hold ourselves and others accountable. It's a strategy for life and work that attracts others to us, because accountability is a universal trait of admired people.

No More Excuses is not a slogan. It is a competitive choice. Whether you are trying to hold onto your job or expand your enterprise, whether you are trying to create a new business relationship or improve your communication with key stakeholders, or whether you are trying to find a new customer or retain a major client, you will always find that personal accountability differentiates you from your competition and give you the competitive edge. Accountability is not a consequence. In order for it to become your competitive advantage, you must be willing to change what you expect from yourself and others.

No More Excuses is all about closing the gap between where we are and where we could be as individuals and as organizations. We can do this by learning and applying, on a personal level, the five critical principles that support an expanding "Accountability Zone" that has us at the very center.

In this book, I will challenge you to expand your own Accountability Zone by embracing what I call the Five Accountabilities:

Right things: Be accountable for doing the right things. This means ethical execution of the activities that will actually support the goals you have chosen for yourself. If you are managing a team, you must model this skill by doing the right things yourself; you must then empower each member of your team to identify his or her own right things, and you must be willing to communicate about what's working and what isn't in an open, transparent way at all times.

New space: Be accountable for managing your space for new opportunities. This means being willing to step away from things that are working, even though they may be familiar, to make room for something that may work better.

Transparency Means Being Accountable for Doing the Right Things—from the Top Down

Organizational governance systems are like machines, and the only oil that actually makes these machines work is the oil of confidence. To generate confidence and trust, you need transparency. If there is no transparency, there is no trust. If there is no trust, the basic architecture of any company just falls down right away.

—Jordi Canals

Yes, this is a risk, but it's one that successful people take—because the return can be positive for the whole enterprise.

Managing your space takes time and practice. Force of habit causes us to repeat many behaviors and initiatives that aren't what we really want.

Process: Be accountable for managing the process when you hit an obstacle. It is inevitable that you will encounter adversities and setbacks when you pursue your goals. The question is, how will the adversities and setbacks affect

---

Redefine Your Space!

If you had the exact same dollars today that you did back then, and knowing what you know now, would you jump into this opportunity or a different one?

—Jeff Booth

How Will You Respond?

We cannot control what happens to us, but we can always control how we react to what happened, and we can always make good choices around what happened.

—Roger Staubach

---

you? Will they keep you from making creative new approaches to attain your goal?

Expectations: Be accountable for establishing the right expectations. The targets you set for yourself will have a huge impact on your actual achievement. How will you set the targets for yourself and your team? Will you set them based on what is familiar or what is possible? Will you set them too high, too low, or in that ideal zone where the goal is a healthy stretch?

Relationships: Be accountable for your relationships and your contributions to them. The human touch in any

---

What Are You Shooting For?

We all have to set our own targets in life. Let's say I'm a student. If all I do is shoot for a B in a course, the likelihood that I am going to get an A is pretty low. If I shoot for an A, even if fall short, I've still got a pretty good chance to get a B. So, I don't want people shooting so low that they create that tyranny of low expectations we've all heard so much about.

—Gerry Czarnkecki

---

relationship is the "lubricant" that makes communication possible and empowers individuals, groups, and organizations to accomplish great things. Without accountability for supporting and contributing to the relationship, there can be no true leadership, and no effective implementation, at the group or organizational level, of any of the other accountabilities.

When you are accountable for supporting and contributing to your relationships, you are acknowledging that there is no such thing as "group accountability"—there is only the accountability of one person to another.

"It's Really about Relationships"

A corporation really is a collection of people. It is a joint mission to accomplish something in a business. The way an organization or a household works, the way a community works—it's really about relationships, and the real measure of any leader is the ability to leverage relationships to influence others to embrace accountability. You can only do that by giving something to your relationships and supporting them over time.

—Peter Aceto

These are the five pillars of personal accountability that make organizational accountability possible. I believe that every truly meaningful achievement and every great organization starts with an *individual* who has established a personal Accountability Zone—a place where the transparency is high, the values are clear, and the commitment to the Five Accountabilities is unmistakable.

These Five Accountabilities are your responsibility before they are anyone else's. What's more, they are *scalable:* They can affect and enhance virtually all aspects of your life, as well as the lives of people you touch. These Five Accountabilities not only transform businesses, organizations, and communities but also help us to improve the larger world we all share.

ARE YOU IN THE ZONE?

When you are in the Accountability Zone, *your actions are fully in harmony with your promises to stakeholders.* I call this *alignment.*

Alignment means being the same person all the time. It means operating with enough integrity to talk straight about both your strategy and your tactics.

What Do You Believe In? What Do You Stand for? What Will You Deliver?

Accountability means being in the position of truly owning all that an organization believes in, stands for, and promises to deliver. Everybody had better be in that position—not just the CEO. The CEO can only deliver on the big picture if the other people in the organization deliver on their pieces of the picture. At the end of the day, everyone is responsible to each other for executing on the larger vision.

—Nido Qubein

When you are in the Accountability Zone, *you know what you're doing and why you're doing it.* I call this *strategic intent.*

You're going to be hearing a lot about strategic intent in this book. Your strategic intent is the driving, overriding goal that motivates and inspires you. It's the goal that everyone gets— not the tactics that support that goal. (Those *tactics* are your right things.) Strategic intent is going to the moon for the first time and getting back safely; it's launching a startup that creates a whole new industry by winning 100,000 new customers in its first year; it's making $250,000 in personal income for the year, when you've never done that before.

Strategic intent is a big goal that's easy to understand *and* buy into.

I created Dean's Beans about 16 years ago for one reason: to model how a for-profit business could be a positive player in social change and still be profitable. That was my strategic intent. So, we were accountable for that social change, whether it was environmental, economic, or social. It was not relegated to the world of the nonprofits. I realized that nonprofits were always asking businesses to give them money, so they could keep going. I made myself accountable for changing the model. I thought, "It's [the] business's responsibility to behave in a way that doesn't damage the earth, the people, [and] the societies in it so that eventually, we can reach a point where those nonprofits may never have to exist." Proving that concept's viability became my own commitment.

—Dean Cycon

When you are in the Accountability Zone, you encourage open dialogue and discussion rather than sealing yourself off from it. I call this *engagement*.

Engagement means connecting with other people. If you're not willing to communicate with people about whatever you're doing that affects them, you are not in the Accountability Zone. Very often, leaders of governments, corporations, and other larger entities must make a special point of identifying at least one individual whose job it is to support the task of promoting dialogue and listening to stakeholders. This engagement may be a little job you can

---

Accountable to a Nation

In our case, we were accountable for creating a new constitution for a post-apartheid South Africa. That meant starting from scratch, disengaging from everything in the old space, and starting a responsible, transparent dialogue that somehow incorporated the views not of a tiny elite [group] but of 42 million people. That dialogue wasn't about revising what had gone before; it was more about liquidating the previous dispensation and replacing it with [a] completely new idea. We had to liquidate the old company as it existed, scrap it and bring it down to zero, and from that create a new environment with a completely new structure. We had to create a new paradigm based on a completely new set of values that would replace an old paradigm that had been in place for 350 years.

—Roelf Meyer

---

do on your own, or it may be something you have to get some help with. After all, some of us have a few stakeholders to listen to, some of us have hundreds or even thousands, and some of us have millions!

When you are in the Accountability Zone, all stakeholders *know what you've done, where you stand, and why.* You are operating above the board. I call this *transparency.*

Most of the high-profile scandals in which business people, politicians, and celebrities find themselves enmeshed come about as the result of an early decision to leave the

---

Be Clear about What's Happening

One of the principles that I live my professional life by—and my personal life, too, for that matter—is to be as open and transparent with people as I can possibly be about what I'm doing and why I'm doing it. I had a conversation with a person who worked for me some time back where I had to deliver some news about a decision I knew he wasn't going to like. After I'd told him what my choice was and how it would affect him, his response was, "Well, I may not agree with your decision, and I may not agree with everything you have always done, but you have always been very clear about what is happening, and I have always understood exactly where you have stood, and that's something I value a great deal in our relationship. I have never had to question where I have stood with you. Thank you for telling me this."

—Richard Chambers

Accountability Zone by keeping key stakeholders in the dark about important choices. This is a seemingly small decision that inevitably echoes larger and becomes more destabilizing over time.

When I'm working with organizations to create a culture of accountability, my clients will sometimes ask: How do we create an Accountability Zone? I think it's more a matter of knowing when you *left* it. Your own private Accountability Zone is always there waiting for you. Here's a quick and easy test you can perform at both the personal and organizational level. If there's no alignment, if there's no engagement, if there's no strategic intent, if there's no transparency—guess what? *You just left your Accountability Zone!*

A better question than "How do I create an Accountability Zone?" is: "How do I *expand* an Accountability Zone?" And the answer is, by making the Five Accountabilities a part of your daily life. In over 30 years of owning businesses, observing people, speaking professionally, and writing, I've found the Five Accountabilities covered in this book to be the most powerful tools for personal and organizational growth available. I suspected that the Five Accountabilities I had identified were already serving as anchors in the lives of the most successful people and organizations on earth. I interviewed dozens of high achievers from around the world and found that they, too, had been using most or all of these principles to create Accountability Zones for themselves and their organizations.

Some of the people I interviewed had mastered the Five Accountabilities quickly in life, almost by instinct; for others, it took years of personal experience and plenty of trial and error to master the principles. No matter how long it takes to master these ideas, no matter what you call them, the lesson remains the same: *The Five Accountabilities work,* if you are willing to use them to change your own life first by expanding your current Accountability Zones and creating new ones as you go along.

This book includes interviews with Highly Accountable People from all walks of life—including corporate CEOs, politicians, professional athletes, educators, a conqueror of Mt. Everest, and even the man who led the effort to write the new constitution of South Africa. These Highly Accountable People came from business, government, and academia, and from six different continents. *They all agreed on the core accountability principles you're about to learn.* As you'll soon see, they have used the Five Accountabilities to open new doors, take advantage of new opportunities, and expand Accountability Zones in their lives, their careers, and their organizations. When you expand your own Accountability Zone, you create and support a culture of accountability within your organization.

No More Excuses gives you the tools you need to go about designing and living an excuse-free life. If you're a

---

Start at the Top

What I have found is that accountability is something that people often don't understand. Leaders have to educate people about what they are accountable for, and the very best place for a leader to start is his or her own management team.

—Sir Andrew Likierman

---

manager or executive, you'll also find insights on the best ways to model the Five Accountabilities for your team. I believe we can all model the highly accountable achievers who have made these five commitments a daily blueprint for living. What's more, I believe that these are the foundation of all great achievements, both on the individual and the organizational levels.

The Key Drivers

When I look at these Five Accountabilities, I think these are probably the key drivers that allow people to make and fulfill commitments.

—George Tamke

The Five Accountabilities have made an incredible difference in my life—and I believe they can make the same kind of difference in your life, too. Let's get started!

How To Use This Book

Expanding your Accountability Zone is as easy as . . .

One: Read chapters one and two. You will get clear on why *accountability matters*, find out how *expensive* the excuses we make to ourselves really are, and get an overview of the *Five Accountabilities* shared by all truly successful people.

Two: then, get serious about the five accountabilities. Each of the following chapters will help you master one of the Five Accountabilities and offers case studies and insights from the Highly Accountable People I interviewed for this book. Lock in what you've learned by completing the Accountability Check activities at the end of each chapter. (You can find additional tools for implementing and reinforcing each Accountability at www.SamSilverstein.com.)

Three! Check Chapter Eight for long-term advice on how to create a culture of accountability within your organization from the remarkable gathering of Highly Accountable People who shared their experiences in this book.

ACCOUNTABILITY MASTERS

The Highly Accountable People who agreed to be interviewed for this book are as follows:

Peter Aceto, President and CEO, ING Direct, Canada

Christine Aquin, President and CEO, Gunpowder Business Development, Inc.

Gary Bailey, Legendary goalkeeper for the Manchester United Soccer Club and a member of the England World Cup Soccer Team

Jeff Booth, President and CEO, BuildDirect

Dixon C. Buxton, Senior Managing Director, Private Capital Corporation

Sila Calderón, Former Governor of Puerto Rico

Jordi Canals, Dean, Instituto de Estudios Superiores de la Empresa (IESE) Business School, University of Navarra

James C. Castellano, CPA and Chairman, RubinBrown

Richard Chambers, President and CEO, the Institute of Internal Auditors

Elim Chew, President, 77th Street

Dean Cycon, CEO, Dean's Beans Organic Coffee Company

Gerry Czarnecki, Former President, UNC Incorporated; Former Senior Vice President, IBM; Former President and CEO, Bank of America Hawaii; Former President and CEO, Altus Bank; Author, *Lead with Love*

Bill Donius, Former President and CEO, Polaski Bank

Mark Eaton, All-star basketball player for the Utah Jazz

Kenneth Evans, Dean, Price College of Business, University of Oklahoma

John Hannah, Former professional football player and member of the National Football League Hall of Fame

Mike Knetter, Dean, Wisconsin School of Business

Lowell Kruse, President and CEO, Heartland Health

Pat Larmon, President and CEO, Bunzl Distribution, Inc.

Peter Legge, CEO, Canada Wide Media Limited

Steve Lipstein, President and CEO, BJC HealthCare

Sir Andrew Likierman, Dean, London Business School

Craig Lovett, Partner/Principal, Incognitus

Achi Ludomirsky, MD, PhD, Director of Pediatric Cardiology, New York University Medical Center

Mariano Macias, President and CEO, Victus, Inc.

Joan Magruder, President, Missouri Baptist Hospital

Brian Martin, CEO and Founder, Brand Connections

Jim McCool, Executive Vice President – Institutional Services, The Charles Schwab Corporation

Roelf Meyer, Director, FeverTree Consulting; Former South African Minister of Defense; Former South

African Minister of Constitutional Affairs and Communication; Former South African Minister of Constitutional Development and Provincial Affairs

Ronnie Muhl, explorer who climbed Mt. Everest

Stan Nowak, CEO, Silverlink Communications

Tan Sri Ramon V. Navaratnam, President, Transparency International, Malaysia

Greg Powell, President and CEO, Fi-Plan Partners

Howard Putnam, Former President and CEO, Southwest Airlines

Dr. Nido R. Qubein, President, High Point University

Dana Roets, Vice President and Head of Operations, Kloof Gold Mine/GFI Mining, South Africa

Steve Romer, Director of Operations, Sydney Convention and Exhibition Center

Peter Schick, Chairman of the Board, Moneta Group

David Silverstein (no relation), CEO, Breakthrough Management Group International (BMGI)

David Snively, Senior Vice President, Secretary and General Counsel, Monsanto Company

Eric R. Spangenberg, PhD, Dean and Maughmer Chair, College of Business, Washington State University

George Steyn, Managing Director, PEP, South Africa

Clem Sunter, Former Chairman and CEO, Anglo American Corporation of South Africa, Gold and Uranium Division

Michael Staenberg, President, THF Reality

Roger Staubach, Former professional football player and member of the National Football League Hall of

Fame; Executive Chairman, Americas, Jones Lang LaSalle Americas, Inc.

George Tamke, Chairman, the Hertz Corporation; Chairman, Culligan, Ltd.; Chairman, ServiceMaster; Former Co-CEO, Emerson Electric; Partner with Clayton, Dubilier and Rice, Inc.

Gareth Taylor, Regional Vice President, Barrick Africa

Dato' Dr. Jannie Tay, Executive Vice Chairman, the Hour Glass

Dr. Beck A. Taylor, Dean, Brock School of Business, Samford University

Paul Taylor, Chairman of the Board, U-Gas/Dirt Cheap

Robert Tuchman, Founder, TSE Sports & Entertainment

Bill Whitacre, President and CEO, J.R. Simplot Company

Pat Williams, Senior Vice President, Orlando Magic

PART ONE

What we are seeing now . . . are the effects of stepping away from accountability, the results of sacrificing long-term survival and success for short-term success. We have to go back to the notion that competence, integrity, and service are worth committing to, because they allow us to deliver value that plays out in the long term.

—Jordi Canals

1

THE $10,000 QUESTION

It was a bright, cold morning in mid-December when one of my best clients called my office. He wanted to check on my availability to speak at his organization's annual leadership conference. My assistant checked the calendar, saw that the date in question was open, and booked the date. We mailed out our standard agreement, and the client signed and returned it.

A couple of weeks later, I realized that a few of my personal commitments had somehow never made it onto my business calendar: little things like my anniversary, spring vacation with my family—and my daughter Jackie's high school graduation! *No problem,* I thought. *We'll just put all the missing items on the calendar.*

When we did, we noticed something interesting.

I was supposed to speak at that favored client's leadership conference in Washington, D.C., at 8:00 on Friday morning, the eighteenth of May. As it turned out, my daughter Jackie's graduation was in St. Louis on the *previous night.* The ceremony started at 7:30 P.M. and wouldn't be over until past 9:30 P.M. When I realized that I had a family commitment on the evening of the seventeenth and a speaking date on the morning of the eighteenth, my stomach started to churn. I'm a frequent flyer, and frequent fliers who live in St. Louis know that the only way out of our fair city after 7:00 P.M. on a Thursday is on a donkey . . . and a donkey definitely wasn't going to get me to D.C. by Friday morning.

I called my client. Here's what I said: "Sal? Hi, Sam Silverstein. How's it going? Good, good. Hey, you know that program in May? Listen, I kind of double-booked myself up against my daughter's graduation. Is there any chance I could speak in the afternoon on Friday or first thing Saturday?"

There was a pause.

Then Sal said, "Sam, let me get clear on something. Your program *is* called 'No More Excuses,' right?"

Now I knew I had a problem. Quickly, I pondered my options. Theoretically—only theoretically, mind you—I could call in sick at the last minute and ask another speaker to come fill in for me. The fact that Sal had branded the entire conference around my signature program "No More Excuses"—was it really that big of an issue?

Yes, it was.

Option number two: I could miss my daughter's graduation. I started thinking to myself, *Well, she is my third child* . . . Then I stopped myself. My stomach started feeling funny all over again. Seriously: There had to be some other answer.

I started calling charter companies to inquire about a flight.

The lowest bidder to get me from St. Louis after graduation to Washington, D.C., in time for my speech was $10,000.

I now had a $10,000 question: *What am I accountable for—and to whom?*

Was I going to pick one commitment over the other, or was I going to write the check? Every time I thought about letting one or the other of those commitments slide, I thought about the guy who'd be looking back at me from the bathroom mirror each morning, and I knew I was going to have to face that guy.

I wrote the check. At about 9:30 P.M. on Thursday the seventeenth, I watched my daughter walk across the stage, with her head held high and a smile that could light up North America, to receive her diploma. At 10:15 P.M., it was wheels up in a little charter plane that might as well have been called "Spirit of St. Louis."

It was a turbulent takeoff. In fact, I remember thinking to myself, *Maybe I **shouldn't** have gone with the low-cost bidder.* But the ride smoothed out nicely, and by about 2:15 A.M., I was tucked away safely between the lily-whites in my hotel room in Washington. I got a couple of hours of shut-eye and made the speech that morning, which was very well received. In fact, I got a standing ovation.

(By the way, the rumor that I made Jackie start her summer job the very next day to help defray the cost of the jet fuel is completely without foundation.)

Here's the point. My $10,000 question wasn't just about Jackie and my client. Ultimately, I realized I had to be accountable *to myself* first in this situation. I had to find a way to follow through on *both* commitments I had made— for them, yes, but for me first. I didn't want to be the kind of person who looked away from either of those commit-ments. Often, as this story illustrates, it takes self-discipline to live our life with ethics, morality, and integrity. Yes, in doing so there will be some late flights and some large bills if you hold yourself accountable. But accepting all of those challenges beats the alternative: making excuses.

That's exactly what I would have been doing if I had gone back on either of those commitments: *making an excuse to myself first*—telling a story, buying it, and then passing that story on to someone else.

I believe that it is only by learning to hold *ourselves* accountable, by taking a pass on the inevitable opportuni-ties we get to feed *ourselves* excuses, that we can achieve the end results we are seeking in life.

A Personal Matter

Accountability is a really deep, personal driver. Even though I believe others can remind you about it and point you toward it, and even though I have certainly had mentors that have done that, I think at the end of the day, it is really up to each individual to make accountability happen.

—David Snively

Eventually, we all face our own version of what I call the $10,000 question. That question isn't really about what kind of flight you take from St. Louis to Washington, D.C. It's about what kind of person you are and what kind of organization you are willing to create by holding yourself accountable first and encouraging others to do the same.

It's about launching your own global *No More Excuses* movement by expanding *your own Accountability Zone.* You have to be the first occupant of that zone, and you have to get very good at stepping back into it once you notice you've strayed from it. Once you've perfected the art of returning to the Accountability Zone as an individual, you've taken the essential first step toward organizational accountability and responsibility.

Individual Integrity, Organizational Integrity

Any discussion of organizational ethics begins with individual accountability, because we all eventually have to pay the consequences when individuals are not accountable to themselves first. If you're not accountable to yourself first, what that means is that you are not honest on the small scale and your integrity is suspect on the small scale. When there's no integrity in individuals, then as the organization scales up and out, it turns out that there is no integrity in processes and organizations, either. We saw that phenomenon with Enron, we saw it with WorldCom, we saw it with Parmalat, and we saw it with some of the devastating risk-management problems that we have encountered in the global economy in recent years. And of course, we saw it in the spectacular scams and frauds that have unfolded, such as the Madoff case. All of those problems are rooted, I think,

(Continued)

(Continued)

in failures of personal accountability. That's what made the organizational problems possible: people who weren't accountable to themselves. We all have to be willing to step back and say, "You know what? This has to start with me, because we all pay the price when we have elements in our culture that are corrosive."

—Richard Chambers

MAKE CHOICES, NOT EXCUSES

I believe that accountability is the basis of all meaningful human achievement. I also believe that our first accountability is to the person we see in the bathroom mirror each morning. No, it's not always easy for us to start there, but it is the very best place for us to start, and it's much, much better to start with accountability to ourselves than it is to start with an excuse.

Ultimately, accountability comes down to choices, the only things we truly own. Everything else that we think we own can be taken away—our home, our cars, all of our possessions. Even the people we know and love can leave us. At the end of the day, the only thing that will remain will be the choices we have made.

To get the most out of this book, *make choices, not excuses, about how to implement and practice what you encounter here.* Conscious choices are the opposite of excuses; they are one of the hallmarks of an excuse-free life.

It's Up To You!

We are each responsible for all aspects of our lives. Many people don't understand that or buy into that. They look for excuses, and they look for other people [to blame]. They think it could be the spouse; it could be the prime minister; it could be the president or the mayor or somebody else who is really responsible. Other people may be responsible for making some decisions that affect us, but ultimately, we are the ones who are responsible for how we respond and how we react. That doesn't mean everything we do is going to succeed, of course, but it does mean we accept full accountability for what is actually happening in our world and for how things work in our lives. I really believe that I am responsible for how Canada Wide works and what I do in the community. That is entirely up to me.

—Peter Legge

MOVING BEYOND THE EXCUSE

What is an excuse? An excuse is a story that you tell yourself to sell yourself—and then try to sell to others. This is an important point: *We always convince ourselves to buy an excuse before we try to sell it elsewhere!*

When I'm speaking to people in my live "No More Excuses" program or working with companies who want to transform their organizational culture to one of pro-active accountability, I encourage people to recite this definition right out loud so that everyone can hear. Why not say it out loud to yourself, too, right now, so that everyone, including you, can hear it?

We must learn to move beyond excuses. The number one reason people succeed in their personal and professional life is that they don't make or accept excuses.

Successful people know that failure is part of the success process. However, they don't use excuses to justify failure, and they don't let others around them get away with excuses, either.

Leaders are accountable. Leaders admit fault. *Leaders do not make excuses.*

Accountability Means Walking the Walk

You've got to walk the walk, and people have to see you walking the walk. If you're going to be accountable as a leader, you've got to spend some time communicating with all of your constituencies. It has got to be interactive. You can get up and make a great speech, and that may be interesting, but after the speech, you have got to be willing to stand up on the stage and interact with people. As the leader, you've got to stay there for as long as you have to [in order to] answer everybody's questions. Interaction is really important, whether it's with your own employees, your vendor base, the people that you have your financial relationships with—it's important with everybody. They all have to understand exactly what you stand for and exactly what they can expect from you. You have got to be willing to get out

(Continued)

in front and listen to what everybody has to say and take the hard questions and give them truthful answers. You have got to be willing to say, "You know what? That's a good question. I don't know the answer, though. I'm going to find out, and I am going to get back to you."

—George Tamke

THE CHERRY TREE

It's interesting to me that a story about accountability has become one of our great tribal narratives in the United States. You know what a tribal narrative is, don't you? It's a story that, even if it isn't true, ought to be.

The story, of course, concerns one of our Founding Fathers, George Washington. Supposedly, after the young Washington cut down a cherry tree, his father approached him and demanded, "Who chopped down the cherry tree?" We're told that Washington responded, "I cannot tell a lie—it was I who chopped down the cherry tree!"

That's accountability. There are *absolutely no excuses* in that response, which may be one of the reasons the story has remained so important to us over the years. Unfortunately, it's a story that a lot of our politicians don't seem to have grasped.

Do you get the feeling that if a politician got in trouble over a cherry tree today, an excuse or two might creep into the equation? I do. In fact, we have a special name for people whose job it is to come up with excuses for politicians. We call them *spin doctors*.

Imagine a president being interviewed today about that same incident.

"Mr. President, did you cut down the cherry tree?"

"Well, yes, and no. It's a complex issue. You see, I couldn't have 'cut it down,' because cutting is actually something one does with a knife. You can 'cut' a finger, but you can't really 'cut' a tree. And since I used my hatchet, the relationship I had with the tree was really not a 'cutting' relationship. Personally, I would call it more of a chopping relationship. And obviously, I didn't cut the cherry tree 'down,' because, as you can see, the cherry tree's stump is still standing. Now, since that stump is clearly a part of the tree, saying that I 'cut down' the cherry tree becomes yet another example of the bitter partisan rhetoric that is poisoning our whole political culture. This an example of an exaggerated claim alleged by those people who have some personal vendetta against me. And after all, the whole reason I approached the cherry tree in the first place was that I was looking for weapons of mass destruction and also looking for ways to avoid having to raise your taxes, which I made very clear during the campaign that I did not want to do. I also want to make this perfectly clear: I—did—not—inhale!"

Don't you hate it when politicians make those kinds of excuses? Me, too. But here's the question: Do we ever let other people get away with them? Do we ever let *ourselves* get away with them? I'm talking about the excuses we use to get ourselves off the hook, deny personal responsibility, and *spin* our own actions so that we can try to manipulate ourselves and other people to accept our own bull.

In the end, excuses are what we use to deny our own personal accountability. And people are finally beginning to realize that denying personal accountability is always at the root of organizational accountability problems.

A New Scrutiny on Accountability

In my lifetime, there has been a huge increase in the requirements for accountability, and here, I mean it in the sense of being answerable. This includes the transparency with which things are done within any organization and the need to report in an open way. Taking two high-profile examples, all the expense claims (including receipts or lack of them) of UK Members of Parliament have been published. As a result, a number have resigned; others have been forced out as some of their more outrageous claims have been exposed. Then, there is the questioning of private-jet travel by automakers on their way to Washington to ask for bailouts but also, more generally, on environmental grounds.

—Sir Andrew Likierman

WHAT ACCOUNTABILITY REALLY MEANS

Accountability means . . . being accountable to ourselves. This is where we should start but usually don't. Accountability to ourselves is what happens when we decide we won't violate our own values, and we resolve to hold ourselves accountable to those values. When I had to choose what to do about Jackie's graduation, I had to find a way to be true to *two* core values: my professional commitments and my responsibility to provide emotional and personal support to my family. Once I realized that I couldn't short-change either of the people I'd made commitments to, my decision was easy.

You already have examples of this kind of accountability in your own life, too. For instance, if you ever had the opportunity to cheat on a test and chose not to, even though no one was looking and you knew you could get away with it, you were holding yourself accountable to your own standards. If you had the opportunity to pad your expense report, but you didn't do that because you didn't want to be the kind of person who cheats on an expense report, you were holding yourself accountable to your own standards.

The question I have for you is this: How often do you hold yourself accountable to your own standards during the average day? Probably more than you think. Don't sell yourself short. If you've ever chosen not to cheat on your diet, even though you could have done so, you know what personal accountability is. If you've ever made a commitment to yourself to get a physical examination from your doctor once a year and followed through on that commitment, you know what personal accountability is. You are already a resident of your own Accountability Zone. Your job now is to make that zone a bigger and more habitual part of your life.

Highly accountable leaders don't simply *impose* accountabilities on the members of their team. They specialize in learning exactly what has to happen for an individual to hold *himself or herself* accountable for attaining a given goal. Yes, this means modeling self-accountability, but it means a lot more than that.

When You Love People, They Become More Accountable

I believe it is our responsibility to help people achieve their own accountability to themselves. This is not a matter of saying, "Hey, you didn't do your job, go get it done." It's not a matter of saying, "By the way, you did a good job back there—you were outstanding, and I am hereby stroking you." We have to accept that at some point, almost everybody is going to have a hiccup, and if we are leaders, it is our job to help them through. Having people accountable to us—managing those accountabilities—carries with it accountability on our side.

We are accountable to support and help the people that we are holding accountable. A lot of executives like to either stroke or punish people, but they don't take the time to develop and support those people. That means these executives tend to reward people who already find it pretty easy to hold themselves accountable for something. That's your A-team. Well, guess what? The world is not made up of superstars. We have A, B, and C players in our organizations. It is our responsibility to help the B and C players move up to the next level. Their personal accountability is something that has to be nurtured and reinforced by our support, and our success or failure as leaders is entirely a result of our ability to empower our people. We are responsible for empowering them to achieve to their fullest potential and become more accountable. Every human being who

(Continued)

> *(Continued)*
> works for me has the capacity and the potential to actualize and to achieve excellence, and it is my job to help them get there.
>
> —Gerry Czarnecki

Accountability means . . . being accountable to other people. This is where we usually start. That's not a bad thing—in fact, it's essential to be accountable to others. When we make commitments to other people, we have to honor those commitments, but if you're not true to your own values, you're eventually going to find it impossible to be true to your commitment to someone else. We must each be the first occupant of our own Accountability Zone.

Which is usually easier for us: Taking action to fulfill a commitment because we're committed to our own values or taking action because we're afraid of what someone else would think? If you're like most of the people I talk to, you'll admit that the opinions of others sometimes play a larger role in motivating you than your own values do. *Are we really more worried about what others think of us than what we think of ourselves?*

Accountability means . . . understanding commitments others have made to us. People may give us excuses. In fact, we may have *trained* them to give us excuses, based on what we have shown we are willing to tolerate in the past. This type of accountability can be very difficult if we're trying to make *No More Excuses* the driving reality in our lives.

We can't buy someone's excuse and stay in our own Accountability Zone. If we're really serious about creating an Accountability Zone, we will occasionally have to confront someone once we receive an excuse. Of course, that is not always easy.

For example, I got a haircut a few months back. The place where I go is a one-man shop that's run by a very nice guy named Bill. I arrived at 9:55 A.M. for a 10:00 A.M. appointment, and the door was locked. Bill didn't show up until 10:30 A.M. As he unlocked the door, he said, "I'm sorry that I'm late. I got a ticket on the way to work."

Have you ever heard that one about the ticket before? How do you respond to that? Do you show sympathy and compassion? Or, do you look for the real issue and then find an appropriate way to call the person on it?

It's easy just to join in the pity party. It's easy to think, "Hey, he got a ticket, cut him some slack." Sometimes we may choose to do that. We should know, however, that *each time we buy an excuse at face value, we leave the Accountability Zone.*

At least half of the time when people let their accountability to us slip away, they're selling us an excuse about something that really happened and hoping we'll buy it without noticing that it didn't really have anything to do with their failure to deliver what they've committed to. I suspected that Bill was going to be late *regardless of whether* he got a ticket but simply didn't mention that part. Was he *planning* to walk in the door at 10:00 A.M.? Wouldn't it have made more sense to *plan* to walk in the door at 9:45 A.M., or 9:30 A.M., to get ready for the day, or just in case something unexpected happened?

The easy way out is to let people who make excuses off the hook—to buy the excuse. But amazing things can happen when you choose not to buy.

I looked at Bill and said, "I know you got a ticket, but you also left late, didn't you?" He said, "Yes."

I left it at that.

The following month, Bill was 10 minutes late (as opposed to half an hour). This time he didn't say a word as he unlocked the door. You see, Bill realized that I didn't want to hear his stories, because his issues are his problems, and they are not my problems. Together, we were building a shared Accountability Zone.

After my haircut, as I was on the way out, Bill said, "Sam, next month I will be standing here waiting for you." And he was. Bill became a better businessman, and I became a better customer, because he chose to move beyond the excuses.

Would we have gotten the same outcome if I had simply bought his initial excuse about the ticket and accepted his poor planning as my problem?

Think twice before you buy or sell an excuse. When you accept an excuse from someone who's made a commitment to you, you take on that person's problem. Don't let someone else's problems become yours, and don't try to offload your problems on anyone else.

Accountability means . . . helping others stay accountable to themselves. This is what happens when people help each other to become more self-accountable. It's part of what I call an Accountability Circle: A group where each person has the implied right to help someone else in the group do a better job of maintaining commitments to themselves. This group is also known as a Mastermind Group. I think everyone should have a group like this. None of us is perfect. Just as we all need a pat on the back from time to time, we all need reinforcement when it comes to creating zones of accountability.

I originally got involved with a Mastermind Group because I thought it was a great way to share ideas and solve problems. I saw it as an opportunity to leverage someone else's experience. What I didn't realize is that there was another, much bigger benefit from the Mastermind Group. It was this: After discussing issues at one of our meetings, each of us would invariably make choices and commit to taking a specific action prior to our next meeting. Coming to the next meeting and not having completed the tasks you'd committed to was simply not acceptable.

This was not a "support group." It was a *choice group:* a place where people went to *make choices, not excuses.* By being part of a Mastermind Group, we each benefited as individuals, and we helped others to become better at being accountable to themselves. We each *expanded our zone of accountability.*

For more information on Mastermind Groups, go to www.SamSilverstein.com.

Our accountability to ourselves makes the other three kinds of accountability possible. It is impossible to create an Accountability Zone in your life without establishing self-accountability. This kind of accountability, I believe, is a prerequisite for all meaningful achievement with the team.

Four hundred years ago, William Shakespeare wrote these words: "This above all: to thine own self be true, and it must follow, as the night the day, though canst not then be false to any man" (Hamlet, I, ll.78–80). Those wise words have been repeated so often and in so many different contexts that we may actually have lost sight of their real meaning. Look at them again. *There's a reason people have been repeating this sentence for over 400 years.* By looking at those words with fresh eyes, by internalizing them, we may find that we have come up against an important opportunity to grow as people.

When we are accountable to ourselves first, when we honor our own values, we really will find it a great deal easier to make and keep commitments for which we can be accountable to others. We'll get better at only making the commitments we can actually keep, and we'll do a better job of following through on those commitments.

When we are accountable to ourselves first and foremost, we will find it's much easier to have productive exchanges with people about areas where there's a gap between what they've promised and what they've delivered.

Last but not least, when we are accountable to ourselves first, we will be a better model and a better resource for the people who look to us for help in building up their own accountability "muscle" and creating their own Accountability Zones.

Of course, I realize that a lot of us find it easier to hold ourselves accountable when we believe we are accountable to others. Consider the following true story.

How Do You Hold Yourself Accountable?

I had a client who was embarking on a big program a few years ago. He called me up one day and said, "Hey Dave, I told the board of directors yesterday that we are going to save $26 million by the end of the year." I said, "That's great, but taking something like that to the board is pretty unusual. Most of my clients don't want to make a big deal out that kind of

(Continued)

> prediction by involving the board. Why did you do that?" He said, "Well, I learned years ago when I was training for a marathon, that by telling my wife, my family, and everyone else about my goals, that is the only way that I can really hold myself accountable. Otherwise, I knew that when I got up to about 16 miles, I would probably quit. By telling other people about what I was going to do, I learned that I hold myself accountable better when I think there are other people watching."
>
> —David Silverstein

It all starts with self-accountability. We live with ourselves 24/7, and if we don't care much about honoring our own values, about following through our own commitments to ourselves, we're going to limit our own potential and needlessly diminish what we can accomplish in this life.

WHAT ARE YOU MODELING?

Are you now committed to *modeling* personal accountability for everyone you meet? If you are, then congratulations: You have just entered the Accountability Zone. Some people spend most of their lives in that zone. Others rarely enter it at all. Which kind of person do you want to be? Where do you want to spend most of your time?

People who make a habit of living in the Accountability Zone know that if they don't model excuse-free standards in their own lives, they cannot possibly receive accountability in return from others. They know that rejecting excuse making is the essential starting point to all mean-ingful achievement. And they know that *buying excuses—* whether their own or someone else's—is an expensive proposition, because they always have to leave the Accountability Zone in order to do it.

Finally, people who spend most of their time in the Accountability Zone know that being accountable is an *active* choice, not a passive response—a choice that enriches all of their relationships and all their outcomes in life.

Remember: Accountability is not a consequence. Accountability is your competitive advantage.

2

Beyond the Excuse

As we have seen, excuses are stories you tell yourself to sell yourself—and then try to sell to others. In this chapter, we look more closely at the habit of selling ourselves excuses and learn why that habit is too expensive.

There are at least three negative outcomes when it comes to using and accepting excuses. Let's look at them.

Consequences

Culturally, we have drifted away from accountability in this country for at least the last generation and perhaps longer. The consequences have been more dire than most people realize.

—Richard Chambers

EXCUSES WEAKEN US AS PEOPLE

I believe that excuses make us weaker as people, *regardless of whether we're giving the excuses or accepting them.* Giving or accepting an excuse is a choice, and choices always have consequences. Often, the consequence is that we get addicted to excuse making.

Have you ever noticed that the most successful people in life do not make very many excuses in the areas that matter most to them nor tolerate many excuses? Have you ever noticed that the *least* successful people in life make a whole lot of excuses and that some of them make a habit of accepting the excuses of others more or less at face value? Do you think that behavior pattern is a coincidence? In my experience, I have learned that *weak people—by that I mean people who are not trying to get the most from themselves— are usually people who are hooked on excuses.*

Donald Trump is successful in business, not *just* because of his business savvy and not *just* because of his family's history in the real estate industry. He's also successful because his personal commitments actually mean something. And you know what else? Another reason he's successful is that he surrounds himself with responsible people, and he doesn't tolerate excuses from them.

Until we can stand up, live our life responsibly, and expect the same responsibility from others that we demand of ourselves; until we are willing to draw a line in the sand when it comes to both giving and receiving excuses and to commit to staying on the right side of that line; until we can say, and mean, "No More Excuses" as our core philosophy in our interactions with ourselves first and others second, we will weaken ourselves with every excuse, and our true potential will evade us.

Truly effective people admit fault when they've made a mistake. They inevitably gain strength by making that admission. Weak people, on the other hand, usually try to attach fault for a problem to someone or something outside of their control, and they always seem to become a little weaker as a result.

Haven't you noticed this? Isn't the person who accepts responsibility for a problem the one who comes out looking and sounding strongest? On the other hand, don't you lose respect for people who deny responsibility for problems that are clearly theirs? And don't those people look and sound stupid when they're in excuse mode?

It is powerful to admit fault without offering a big excuse story, but we rarely hear people do this. We rarely hear people say,

"Yes boss, I was late, and it won't happen again."

"Yes officer, I was speeding, and I deserve a ticket."

"Yes senator, I sold energy to California for exaggerated prices and absconded with shareholder money."

That's not what we hear. What do we hear instead? Some variation of "It's not my fault," when everyone knows that it really is. As a result, we get sick of "It's not my fault" whenever *we* hear it.

And you know what? We have a *right* to be sick of it. We've heard "It's not my fault" for far too long. We want to live in a world where people actually own up for things like getting to work late, acting unethically, or breaking the law. Personally, I'm still waiting for some of those steroid users who hit all those home runs to stand up and say what they did was wrong for themselves, for Major League Baseball, and for the country as a whole.

Don't we all want to live in a world where people admit what happened, take responsibility, and fix the problem?

Don't we all want to live in a world where people grow up, step up, and own up?

If we really want to live in that world–and I have a feeling that deep down, all of us do—then we have to make some changes in our own life. We have to *accept that excuses only make us weaker* as individuals, as organizations, as a nation, and as a species on this planet. And we have to be willing to stop making and accepting excuses in our own life.

Are we really losing all that much when we commit to stop making excuses? I don't think so. The main thing I can see that we're losing out on is the opportunity to look and sound just as stupid as all the excuse-makers out there. This opportunity to distinguish ourselves is something we should actually be grateful for, because the act of making excuses makes us look stupid—and you can't fix stupid.

A motorist once explained the reason she got into an accident in the following unforgettable words: *As I approached the intersection, a sign suddenly appeared in a place where no sign had ever appeared before, making me unable to avoid the accident.*

Do we really want to be known as the kind of person who comes up with that sort of lame excuse? I don't think so.

I believe we each have a responsibility to be *proactively accountable* in what we do. That means we stop spending time and energy making excuses for what has happened in the past, and we start building ourselves and others up as people by making clear commitments for what we will be delivering in the future.

Reactive accountability is about managing the past. When you manage the past, you are unable to create the present or future you desire. To live a prosperous present and create an ideal future, you must use proactive accountability. It is only through proactive accountability that you take control of what you should really be focused on and insure that you achieve what you desire in the future.

Just saying "my bad" without drawing any conclusions about what should take place in the future is reactive accountability. That is the sound of weakness. Proactive accountability uses the past as a guide and establishes exactly what we are committing to from this point forward. For instance, if we had avoided the temptation to blame traffic signs and instead stopped risky behaviors like talking on the cell phone while we were driving, that would have been an example of proactive accountability. We cannot be proactively accountable if we have become addicted to giving or accepting excuses.

Here's the good news. A lot of the people who *do* build their lives around giving and accepting excuses are the people who are working for our competition. Let's face facts: *It doesn't take all that much to distinguish ourselves from these people.*

- If you show up, you're in the top 25 percent. That's if you just show up!
- If you show up with a plan, you're in the top 15 percent.
- If you show up with a plan and you work that plan, you're in the top 10 percent.
- If you show up with a plan, work that plan, don't make excuses, and are proactively accountable, you're in the top 5 percent. From there, you can succeed in almost anything you do.

Learn to stop making and accepting excuses. You will enter that top 5 percent and become stronger as a person. Why? First and foremost, you will stop making excuses *to yourself.*

It is far easier to make excuses to ourselves than we realize. Do you know the number one excuse people give for not going to the gym to exercise? *The gym is too crowded.*

Stop and think about that one for a minute. "Gee, I know I ought to go to the gym, but it's awfully crowded at this time of day." McDonald's gets crowded, too, but we don't seem to have a problem with waiting in *that* line! We give ourselves too many excuses, and the result is that we get weaker—physically, emotionally, spiritually— each and every time we buy into our own excuse or someone else's.

EXCUSES PUT THE FOCUS ON THE STORY

Again, excuses are *stories* we make up about why we believe we are not responsible, when we know we actually are. Every time we make or accept an excuse, we put our energy and attention into The Story, we lose transparency in the relationship, and our values slip. Eventually, if we're not careful, The Story—not our own guiding values and not our strategic priorities—becomes the way we make it through the day.

We seem to think that if The Story is good enough, there's not really any problem. Guess what? No matter how good The Story is, we still haven't fixed the problem!

We as a society are spending way too much time on The Story and way too little time on doing what we ought to be doing with our lives. Have you ever heard that great song by the Eagles, "Get Over It"? It's all about people who have talked themselves into believing The Story and who can't think of living any other way than repeating it over and over.

Let me ask you a question: Have *you* ever come up with a creative story for coming in late to work? Even once?

Making excuses puts all the energy and focus on The Story and no focus, with no energy, on the situation at hand. The Story never makes you a better team player, a better leader, or a better contributor. The Story undermines your abilities and ultimately, your self-esteem.

So, for instance: If you're in sales, when you don't make the sale, stop coming up with a new, intricate story blaming the client. You know the kind of story I mean:

"They misled me every step of the way . . . they never really gave me a shot . . . they deliberately wasted my time . . . they couldn't make up their mind . . . they had this sweetheart deal with the competition that they didn't tell me about . . . "

You will never be a better salesperson if you don't take responsibility for the end result. Either they bought it, or they didn't. Period. You're not getting paid to write The Story about why they didn't buy. No one gets hired to come back with excuses—or a trunk load full of product.

When we choose to focus on The Story, we get so caught up in arguing for our limitations that we actually accept them as reality. We focus on The Story and not the solution, so we never fix the problems that are actually holding us back.

It is only when we face the facts and eliminate the excuses that we discover the answers to our questions, the solutions to our challenges, and the behaviors that will ultimately deliver the kind of business and life that we want and deserve.

Eventually, we have to stop and ask ourselves: What is our story—our excuse—going to cost us? Accountable people realize that the price is almost always too high.

For example, I run marathons. When I'm running a 26-mile-long race, I hear a lot of excuses in my head. I may have cramps in my side, my knees may ache, and I may be exhausted. I may even start wondering whether the vacation money I spent to come torture myself in this marathon would have been better spent on a chaise lounge and a cold beer overlooking a beautiful beach in Cozumel. There comes a point as I'm running a marathon when I begin to hear "quit." And it's at that point that I have to decide whether I'm going to listen to all the reasons for quitting that my mind can come up with.

It's at that point that I have to decide whether I'm going to buy into my own stories. It's a question of whether you're looking for reasons to sell yourself an excuse or reasons not to.

That's what happened to me in my first Boston Marathon. By mile five of the race, I had killer cramps, and at one point, I was bent over and in pain by the side of the road. I could have bailed out; there were plenty of reasons I could have given myself—plenty of stories I could have told myself—to support the idea of quitting. I pulled myself together and kept running. I saw myself crossing the finish line.

At mile 7.7, when you leave Framingham, Hanson Electric is on the right side of the road. Hanson Electric is a single-story building with reflective plate glass windows. Old Man Hanson stands in front of the store, and using a bullhorn, yells, "Check yourself out in the window; check out your form as you run by!"

If you see your form in the window and you look good, it could be a comfortable 19 miles to the finish line. I really didn't want to look. I knew how bad I felt. But I peeked out of the corner of my eye, anyway.

It was worse than I thought.

Now, Old Man Hanson must have seen me and taken pity, because the next thing I heard was, "Don't worry. Objects in window may look worse than they really are."

So, now I had evidence for another story if I wanted it. *Who am I kidding? I not only feel awful, I look awful. Maybe I didn't train correctly. Maybe I'd better stop after all.* I got out of excuse mode and kept running. I saw myself crossing the finish line.

At about mile 12, you're running up Route 135, right past Wellesley College. Wellesley is one of the nation's great all-women's schools, and there's a tradition of supporting the Marathon. Suddenly, there are thousands of women lining the street to cheer you on. As I ran by, I looked around and thought: *You know what? This would be a great place to pause . . . for a semester or two!* Another possible story flashes through my mind: *Hey, I made it all the way to Wellesley. That's a pretty good effort. Maybe that's good enough.* I was tempted, but I put that story aside and kept running. I saw myself crossing the finish line.

At mile 15, there was a table with cups of water for the runners, and I knew I needed water really badly, but the table was so crowded that I decided not to stop. Before I passed the table, though, I felt a spray of water on my back. Someone must have seen that I needed the water and just thrown it out at me. I looked back in gratitude. It was a Catholic priest. I think he was giving me the last rites!

I kept running. I saw myself crossing the finish line.

When we eliminate the excuses, we don't even deal with them. We don't evaluate whether they're good excuses or bad excuses. We just keep moving forward. The only thing ahead of us is the finish line. Once we are truly accountable, we stop giving energy to the stories, because we recognize that we have *no more excuses* for not achieving at an extremely high level.

I am proud to be able to tell you that I crossed the finish line that day. And the reason was actually pretty simple: I didn't give any energy to the stories that were looking for a place to land in my head.

There always comes a point where we have a choice. We can focus on the excuse, The Story—all the reasons why things shouldn't happen—or we can focus on the finish line. When we choose to focus on the excuses, we take ourselves out of the game. If we focus our attention on the finish line rather than on our excuses, then that's where we'll end up: crossing the finish line.

EXCUSES LIMIT OUR EXPERIENCES AND HORIZONS

Excuses *legitimize* the past, *ignore* the present, and *eliminate* the future. That adds up to a big *lie*!

Be honest: What are we really doing when we toss out a lame excuse or accept someone else's? We're throwing a pity party. Excuses are a plea for sympathy when things aren't going precisely our way. Here's the part we sometimes forget: We are just as much a part of the pity party when we buy into someone else's excuse!

Things are going so badly for me. I'm crying, and you should be crying, too. I never get the luck I need. I'm not reaching my sales goals. My company's pricing structure is too high. The economy isn't doing what I want it to do. My parents made me eat lima beans when I was little!

It takes two to tango. And it definitely takes two to form a pity party.

Now hear this: There are five, and only five, things in life that you need to do to be a success. I'll show you what they are in the next section of this book. I can tell you here and now, though, that throwing a pity party or accepting an invitation to one *definitely isn't one of those things.*

Sometimes, we make up our own excuses for accepting less than we deserve. Sometimes, we accept other people's excuses and use theirs to do the same thing. Either way, we lose, because excuses limit our experiences in life and *condition* us to accept less than we deserve. All too often, our excuses keep us living a very small life and stop us from experiencing some really great things. Excuses give us a reason to say no to our own potential and close the window on our own strategic intent.

It is *only* when we create a culture of accountability within our team or our organization that our strategic intent can be realized!

PART TWO

Everybody has a great plan. The plans are masterful. The plans capture the essence of the challenges in the marketplace. The plans recognize the company's strategic position. The plans take all the competitive challenges into account. If it were just a matter of coming up with a great plan, success would be a very simple matter. The problem is, leaders don't execute the damn plan, and they don't hold people accountable. So we go in and turn things around, and what we do is not magical. It is just a matter of saying, "Okay, let's review what the plans were, and let's understand what the commitments that connect to that plan are, and let's follow through and manage the thing in all the details." It is setting the expectations properly so that the commitments that people make do have meaning and are realistic. You have to instill in the organization a sense of responsibility, so that the word commitment has meaning. Then you reward those people who demonstrate commitment, and you get rid of those people who don't."

—George Tamke

3

THE FIRST ACCOUNTABILITY: DOING THE RIGHT THINGS

Efficiency, as Peter Drucker once said, is doing things right; effectiveness is doing the right things. Doing the wrong things in an efficient way can cost us. When we look closely at any given day of our lives, we realize we might be doing the fun things, and we might be doing the easy things. Are we sure, though, that we're doing the *right* things?

Little Things Can Have a Big Impact

One of the things that climbing Mt. Everest does for you is help you get very clear about what you should be doing and what you shouldn't be doing. Because so much of what you do has such direct impact on whether you live or die, you *have* to do the right

(Continued)

> *(Continued)*
> things, and you have to do that consistently—or you die. Something as simple as putting one foot in front of the other, you realize, carries tremendous consequences. It can't be any step; it has to be the right step. That lesson really hit home for me. The mountain gave me the opportunity to learn the importance of the little things that you do, because the little things have big implications. It's an intense way to live, but it's a good way to live, I think. You get into the habit of asking yourself, "If my life depended on the next action I took, how differently would I perform that action?"—because doing the wrong thing can have massive consequences. When a single action can determine whether you live or die, you learn to evaluate your actions a little more closely.
> —Ronnie Muhl

"WHAT MAKES YOU SUCCESSFUL?"

Some years back, I had lunch with someone whose achievements in life and business I really respected, and I asked him a blunt question: "What makes you successful?" His answer was a simple one: "Do the right things consistently, and do them with a commitment to excellence."

I've never forgotten that answer, and every successful person I've interviewed for this book has agreed with it. We are each accountable for doing the right things consistently in life. If something is not working at the level of excellence for us, that fact is our responsibility and no one else's. No one else can do our own right things for us. And no one can ensure that we are doing them to the level of excellence if we do not.

By "doing our own right things for us," I mean choosing those activities that support our strategic intent. Once we have settled on a goal that makes sense for us, we must be relentless in pursuing the answer to this question: *What can I do consistently, with a commitment to excellence, that will make it easier to achieve this goal sooner rather than later?* We must pose this question for ourselves as individuals and for any people who are looking to us as a leader.

Execution and Results

Without exception, anyone in a leadership role has to stand tall and accept the responsibility for not only setting the vision but also for establishing the strategy, for the execution, and the results.

—Nido Qubein

Sometimes people say to me, "Sam, it sounds inspiring, but how do I start? What do I actually do? What happens if I don't know what my own 'right things' are? What if my team doesn't know?" One good way to start when it comes to doing the right things is to benchmark others and find out what *their* right things are. Looking at what others are doing to get results that are similar to the ones you want to get in your own life can be a great reality check. Call people up and take them out to lunch (like I did). Ask them, "What are you doing?"

Writing this book has been a truly great experience for me in terms of implementing and reinforcing this critical first level of accountability. Why? Because it's forced me to reach out to dozens of highly successful people for interviews. Those interviews have allowed me to get multiple reality checks on the right things that these people are doing in their everyday lives, day in and day out. In fact, I've learned more about doing the right things in the last six months than I learned in the previous six years.

But I had to take the initiative. I had to reach out to people and *ask* if they'd share what they'd learned about accountability in their own lives and then *ask* them for specific examples of right things that worked for them in supporting their accountability to a big goal. Contrary to what you might think, I found that the *more* successful people were, the *more* willing they were to share their "do the right thing" stories with me. Getting in touch with people in the first place sometimes takes a little persistence; and no, wrestling your way onto their calendar isn't always easy. But once you connect and once you get people talking, you get ideas and insights on what the right things look like, how to refine them, and how to execute them in your world at a level of excellence.

Right Tools, Right Things

Doing the right things, for me, is always based in maximizing my strong suits. When I started my company, I knew my worst attribute was cold calling, and my best attribute was meeting people in social situations and developing a relationship that way. I played to my strong suits in business, just as I had in the NFL.

(Continued)

That's a big part of doing the right things—knowing what you do best and emphasizing those things to support your goals. You are the one who has to be accountable for managing that process.

There was a time when I was with the Patriots when I was getting beaten by a defensive lineman by the name of Joe Klecko—a great player and a great guy. Joe was controlling what was happening and making me look bad. On the sidelines, I got frustrated. I knew I was trying too hard, and my frustration was growing. My coach sat me on the bench and told me to calm down. He said something I'll never forget: "Sit here and *think* about what he's doing to beat you and what you need to do to stop him. He's not better than you. You're just using the wrong technique. In any given game, you have to have a toolbox full of techniques. As the competition changes what they do, you have to have an assortment of tools you can use to adapt to the situation."

—John Hannah

John Hannah is a Hall of Famer, and I believe that a big part of the reason for that is his willingness to put the emphasis exactly where it belongs: on *refining* what he was doing so that he could execute at the level of excellence in a way that supported his goals. Doing the right things means taking responsibility for changing your techniques and adding new techniques to your toolbox. Whenever I'm asked for an example of doing the right things, John's story is one of my favorite case studies. You don't have to be a football player to get this concept!

41

Another great example of doing the right things with a commitment to excellence—and one that I love to share with people from all walks of life—comes from the world of sales. And no, you don't have to be a salesperson to get it!

Some sales managers (in fact, most sales managers) fall into an unfortunate trap. They get hooked on counting which "closed deals" have come in the door over the last week; they get addicted to comparing that number to the team quota, the number their department is supposed to hit. That's as far as they look: "What's come in recently, and how does it match up with the quota for this month?" (Or, even worse: "How does it match up with the quota for this quarter?")

Some sales managers take a more tactically sound approach; they ask, "What activities have been proven to *lead* to sales, and what's the daily quota for *those* activities?" Once the sales manager knows the answer to that question—once he or she has concluded for certain that X number of conference calls with decision makers at the CFO level or above leads to Y number of new customers over Z period of time—that sales manager doesn't get distracted by the number of deals coming in the door today.

Yes, you read correctly. I said "distracted." Great sales leaders know that it's the consistent relationship-building activity within the pipeline *over time* that matters, not the deals that come in the door on any given day—like, for instance, the Tuesday before the quarter ends. Show me a sales team that's worried about what closes today, and I'll show you a sales manager who hasn't figured out how to get the team to take control of the *right things* in their own sales process.

There is a significant tactical difference between maximizing short-term sales and sustaining long-term growth. When you've taken control of the right things that need to happen day in and day out in your own process, you know you're going to hit quota. Why? Because your right things— the number of calls you need to make, the number of meetings you need to conduct, the number of face-to-face proposals you need to deliver—are already keyed to your goal. It doesn't come as a surprise to you that you need to make X number of conference calls to hit your goal for the quarter, and you don't start thinking about that March 31 goal on the first day of March! Because you had a good sales manager, a sales manager who was doing something besides measuring the deals that came in the door *today,* you were focused on doing your own right things on the very first day of the year.

Some sales managers call these *right things* Key Performance Indicators. That name works for me as well as any other. Whatever name you use, though, you must hold *yourself* accountable for identifying them, executing them with excellence, and measuring these activities, day in and day out. In other words: *If you sell for a living, don't get distracted by the sales that come in the door today!* Not closing a deal today isn't all that big of a deal if you've been doing the right things to support your selling goal for the past month; *closing* that deal today may actually take your eye off the ball. If you "celebrate" that deal by taking three weeks off from doing the right things, you'll eventually be sorry.

How Are You Using Your Leadership Bandwidth?

I think one of the scarcest resources in business is not financial capital, not human capital, but leadership bandwidth. This is always tied to the leader's ability

(Continued)

(*Continued*)

to focus on the right things, and tune out everything else. Many companies have gotten so big that they lose track of their own resources, and the resource that they underestimate most is their own leadership bandwidth. The company is just too complicated and there are just too many things to do for anyone to do them all well. So, eliminating things that are on your to-do list and knowing how to prioritize and focus on the strategic imperatives— that skill is something that is especially good for you. It's something we all have to hold ourselves accountable for. If you let yourself get dragged into the minutia— if you are constantly being a micromanager— the micromanaging rolls downhill. If you micromanage your executives, guess what? They now have to micromanage *their* team. All of a sudden, you are sucking up all of this leadership bandwidth, and the company can't do the things that it needs to do.

—David Silverstein

KNOW YOUR RIGHT THINGS!

Knowing what your own unique right things are is something you do day by day—and it's also the work of a lifetime. The goal is to identify the things we do best that support our goals and then come back to those right things again and again, relentlessly. This is our job and no one else's. Once we accept our own accountability for executing our own right things, we'll find it much easier to distinguish our organization, and ourselves, from competitors.

Get Specific!

One of my right things is *focusing*—identifying and owning a very specific area of expertise. This is important in a crowded marketplace. It's a tactic I share with clients and one I use to build my own business. When I quit my job and started this company, I knew I had to stand for something specific in the market. I had to choose one particular thing, own it, live it, and become that brand. If I wanted to be well known in an environment where there were a lot of people doing similar things to what I was doing, I had to find a niche. So, I did what I told my clients to do: I focused. I built my business around developing marketing tools for national brands to help them reach consumers at a specific time: while they are in travel and leisure environments. That positioning was super focused; it's what got people to think of me as "the guy who can reach people while they are relaxing on vacation." That one tactic allowed me to break through all my other competitors and own a place in people's minds, so I could build my brand.

—Brian Martin

ARE YOU SLEEPWALKING?

I believe that most of us really do know the right things we're supposed to be doing. The problem is that it's so easy to overlook those right things. We get in the office in the morning and we might as well be sleepwalking through the day.

We spend an hour looking at our inbox in a trance state or maybe listening to some juicy office gossip that has nothing to do with what we should really be doing with our day. How much time do we spend in trances dealing with stuff like e-mail, gossip, or some other unimportant "business"? So much time that we don't want to measure it? That, my friend, is too much time.

So, what do we do? We try to be proactive. We pull out our legal pad and list all the stuff that we think we need to do. Can you guess what the first thing on that list is going to be, nine times out of 10? Right: the *easiest* thing to do. It's not the most important or possibly even the most urgent thing, and it doesn't really connect to our goal for the day, but we do it anyway, because it's the easiest, and we want to get that all-important first check mark of the day so that we can feel like we've accomplished something.

We've got to wake up! Once we wake up, we will find that at some level, we really do know what we're supposed to be doing with our day—and with our lives. And then we can start doing it.

Time Is the Critical Resource

Doing the right things consistently is a tactical way of delivering on your plan, and it starts with you as a manager or as an executive. The most critical commodity that you have as an executive or as a CEO running a business is your time. Where you choose to spend your time is the most important decision you make every day, every week, every month. If you use your time to work a number of wrong things, you are screwed.

—George Tamke

It is time for us get serious about this: *We and we alone are accountable for how we spend our time.* We like to pretend sometimes that other people, other institutions, or other events can determine how we use that resource. That's a fantasy. No one else decides what we're going to do with our day. It's us!

What Really Matters?

You have got to be pretty selective as to what you get engaged in; otherwise, you get burned up with the crisis of the moment as opposed to thinking in the long term. You have to stay focused on what really matters. In my office, I keep a list of what I consider the top 10 things that I have got to work on for the 12 months to come, and I update that list and revise it regularly. I come back to that list every day just to make sure I am grounded in what really matters.

—David Snively

All too often, we invest our time, effort, and energy on tactics that do not necessarily support our strategic intent, or indeed, any strategic intent whatsoever. We are building our day around tasks that are not really crucial to our mission; they are just "urgent."

Urgent or Important?

Here's an experiment: Take something that you think is urgent, and see whether you think it's actually
(Continued)

> *(Continued)*
> *important* to do that thing. See what happens when
> you try to eliminate the urgent and focus on the impor-
> tant. Most people stay so busy doing the urgent stuff
> that they never get around to doing the important stuff.
> —Dixon Buxton

It is all too easy to get stuck with someone else's priorities, someone else's to-do list, and someone else's assump-
tions about what supports the mission. If we are truly
accountable to ourselves, we will confirm for ourselves
what supports our strategic intent and what doesn't.

Improvising Your Way toward the Right Things

I didn't know I wanted to be in the sports event
business; I just knew that I wanted to be in sports,
and I wanted to be doing something I loved.

Eventually, I read about a sports publishing company
that was based in Chicago, and I landed a job with them
and worked selling advertising space out of my home
in New York. What I realized was that the people buying
the ads were much more interested in getting the tickets
I was offering as a premium than in buying the ads!
At that point, I realized that I was looking at a real business opportunity. It wasn't selling advertising—a lot of
places were doing that. Getting people *into* sports
events was the real value. Shortly after that, my partner
and I started our corporate event business.

(Continued)

My goal was big enough to leave me some flexibility. Sometimes, as you pursue a goal, you come across an opportunity that doesn't look like an opportunity to other people. You're basically improvising your way toward finding new right things that will work for you.

There weren't a lot of companies trying to do what I wanted to do, which was build a business around sports events travel packages. Over the years, as my business has grown, the industry has grown as well, and there are a lot more precedents to follow now. Back then, I was definitely improvising a lot and always looking for new right things that would move me toward my goal.

Who's going to change what you're doing, so you end up doing something that *does* work, if it's not you?

—Robert Tuchman

Robert Tuchman's experience is a classic one among entrepreneurs. He had a stable job at Lehman Brothers but found he could not commit in the long term to that organization's strategic intent. He found his own strategic intent and his own right things to support it. He ended up launching a company. The career he left behind at Lehman Brothers turned out to not be as stable as everyone thought. The company eventually collapsed. Robert's company, on the other hand, is doing great!

STRATEGIC INTENT

How do we know what our own right things are? By asking a critical question: Is what I am doing right now supporting my own *strategic intent?*

People often ask me, "What is strategic intent?" Strategic intent is nothing more or less than *a driving goal, passion, or purpose that we are motivated to pursue at the level of excellence.*

This kind of intent operates in two dimensions: the individual dimension and the organizational dimension. In either case, if you're not pursuing your goal at the level of excellence, *you are not pursuing your strategic intent.* That's because strategic intent is inherently competitive. We're not just accountable for identifying the right things that will help us execute on any plan; we're accountable for identifying the right things that allow us to excel. Unfortunately, most people do not pursue these right things or even bother to learn what they are.

What Fills Your Space?

I've always been a believer in the idea that if you're not clearly focused on your goal as an individual, an organization, or a company a million things will come up to fill the space.

—Bill Donius

Sometimes, people call anything and everything they're doing, in order to pursue their goal, their "strategy" to attain what they want. In fact, these activities are *tactics*. Your strategy is your driving goal; your tactics are the things you do to turn that goal into reality. By definition, all things that fall into the category of right things are tactics that support your strategy.

Where Will You Get the Greatest Positive Result?

The first step is defining a good strategy by setting the right kind of goal. Then, you have to ask: How do I ensure that I'm really carrying this out? You have to focus in on where you will get the greatest result. In our strategic planning, that's exactly what we do. Each of my associate deans has to tell me the four things he or she is working that will have the biggest positive effect when it comes to achieving the larger goal for that person's program.

—Mike Knetter

STRATEGIC INTENT: THE INDIVIDUAL DIMENSION

On the individual level, strategic intent is that which you are personally most committed to making happen in your life at the level of excellence. If you don't yet *know* what you are committed to making happen at a peak level in your life, you have some work to do in determining what really matters to you as an individual, and I'm afraid only you can do that work.

I learned from interviewing John Hannah that his strategic intent was to become the best offensive lineman in the National Football League. He achieved that goal. How did he do it? In part, by using a single stance to throw off his opponents about what he was planning to do on the next play. He also pursued that goal by studying game films for hours on end so that he could uncover opportunities that (in Robert Tuchman's words) didn't look like opportunities to most people.

That turned out to be one of his right things. It aligned with his personal goal of being the best offensive lineman the NFL, and it was something he was willing to pursue and execute at the level of excellence.

What is your strategic intent as an individual? It *might* be becoming the best lineman in the NFL, but the odds are that you're going to point yourself in a different direction. When you know for certain what your own strategic intent is—and not before—you'll be ready to start figuring out whether you're doing the right things that *support* that intent.

Evaluate your strategic intent and the things you are doing to support it on a regular basis.

Don't Wait!

I have known plenty of people who thought they were doing fantastic jobs, only to discover that the people around them didn't. This is a big mistake if one of the people is your boss or (if you're the boss) your board or shareholders. Don't wait for the year-end to find out. Keep it in your mind all the time and get feedback before it is too late.

—Sir Andrew Likierman

STRATEGIC INTENT: THE ORGANIZATIONAL DIMENSION

On the organizational level, which we may also be account-able for, the strategic intent is that which our *company* pursues at the level of excellence. Hopefully, that's obvious from the organization, but organizational goals, like individual goals, may be poorly defined—or not defined at all. If we know the direction our organization is headed and are committed to excellence in achieving, our right things will always connect to our company's driving purpose—assuming that we share in that mission as stakeholders.

Are You Aligned with Your Own Agenda?

We have an organizational goal of being in the top 5 percent of all hospitals in the country for quality, for safety, for patient satisfaction scores, for financial stability, and for our employee satisfaction. We know those are attainable targets. There are benchmarks that are out there that support those goals. So, we are able to ask ourselves, "Are we moving with the agenda? Are we aligned with it?"

—Joan Magruder

Herb Kelleher established the strategic intent of Southwest Airlines very early on in his tenure as the leader of that airline. He wanted to make Southwest the number one low-fare airline in the United States—no ifs, ands, or buts. That was his mission and the company's mission. For CEOs and other executives, the individual's strategic intent sometimes fuses with the organization's strategic intent.

There's a great story that people tell about Herb's obsessive focus on strategic intent. One day, an employee came into Herb's office and said, "Mr. Kelleher, we've done a poll of our passengers, and we've found out that the people who regularly fly the Las Vegas to San Francisco route would like to have a nice chicken salad sandwich served to them during the flight. What do you think?"

Herb said, "I've got a question for you: Does serving a chicken salad sandwich get us measurably closer to being the number one low-fare airline in the United States?"

The employee thought for a moment and then said, "No, I guess it doesn't." Herb took a pass, and so should you when you come into contact with any initiative that doesn't support your organization's strategic intent. That's not your right thing! What specific activities will keep an organization on track with its strategic intent? What activities won't? What specific activities will keep a community, a nation, or an employee base on track with a given strategic intent? What activities won't?

Change the Behavior!

What we're seeing in this country is a movement toward doing the right things when it comes to health and wellness. That movement is being led by employers and by some innovative health plans that are beginning to reward healthier behaviors in meaningful ways. Health plans are starting to design benefits based on specific behaviors— specific right things that will keep people healthier over time. You know, that's really exciting, because it benefits a lot of constituencies, and it has a very significant positive impact on health care costs. So, when employers and health care providers start to assume accountability for that, employees follow suit and begin to assume accountability for

(Continued)

---

changing those behaviors. The employers model the right things for their employees, and that brings about a new focus on the right things at the individual level. Why is this important? Because the *Journal of Occupational and Environmental Medicine* reports that 70 percent of health care costs in this country are lifestyle related and are largely driven by behavior. In 2008, U.S. annual health care costs topped $2.4 trillion. If 70 percent of this $2.4 trillion annual spending is related to our health behaviors, it's clear that the ability to drive these behaviors is a significant opportunity for our country to reduce healthcare costs and to improve health outcomes.

—Stan Nowak

STRATEGIC INTENT IS MANDATORY!

You must have a clear strategic intent from both an individual perspective and from an organizational perspective if you hope to identify and execute the right things that support your goals. Don't pick a dozen *different* strategic intents.

If you or anyone on your team can't remember your strategic intent, it's too complicated!

"WHO OWNS THIS?"

Once you've identified the big goals, figure out who's doing what to turn that goal into reality. A big part of organizational accountability is knowing who owns the right things that connect to that goal. Get used to asking, *"Who owns this?"*

Certainty

When I think about accountability, I think of it as the certainty of accomplishing previously set goals. If I'm held accountable or if I'm holding somebody else accountable, I want to be absolutely certain that they have accomplished what we have agreed upon as our previously set goals. And there has to be clarity on both sides for that to happen. That's why accountability always reverts back to the clarity of your strategic planning and your vision.

A common problem with strategic planning is a lack of focus. Sometimes people walk out of the planning process with 10 or 15 different initiatives that they're supposed to follow through on. Our experience is, when you get more than two or three initiatives in a given year, or four at the most, there's just no way you're going to accomplish them, because it's impossible to keep track of them. So, when we do our strategic planning, we make sure we walk out of the strategic planning process with no more than two or three major initiatives. And then, we create responsibility for those initiatives. Who's going to do this? Is it a committee? Is it an individual? Is it the whole group? And we agree to what the action item is going to be for accomplishing that particular initiative.

—Peter Schick

Identifying our own strategic intent is *mandatory* if we hope to identify the right things for ourselves or our organization or to revise those right things over time as circumstances demand. And this, of course, is one of the big challenges managers face. Ultimately, within any organization, it is the manager's responsibility to ensure that the right things that are in place are appropriate, not only to the organization's strategic intent but also to the changing circumstances that must inevitably be accommodated.

For each of us, the right things may vary, given our individual skills and the nature of the changes our teams encounter, but those will always have the goal in sight.

For me, the right things might be to review my own strategic plan and measure progress, to reach out to new prospects, to deliver a certain number of speeches, to build relationships with key executives, or to write a new article for my monthly business, ezine. That all supports the strategic intent I have of growing my business to a certain level. For the people in my organization who I manage, I am accountable for synchronizing my company's strategic intent with *each* team member's skills, aptitudes, and interests. This means that each member of the team may—and typically does—pursue a unique array of right things. If I were to pretend that all of my employees were identical and had the same skills, aptitudes, and interests so that I could assign the same right things to each and every team member, I would be letting everyone down. I would be overlooking my accountability to them to identify the right things that would allow them to make headway on our shared goals, so I couldn't be too surprised if they did not make headway. Some people are better writers than others. Some people are better salespeople than others. Some people are better administrators than others. The key is to develop a list of right things that plays to each team member's strength.

Giving ourselves the very best list of right things to do means knowing our own strong suits and adjusting accordingly, based on our strategic intent and our current circumstances. I've found that people who are personally accountable to themselves, first and foremost, have a way of mastering this skill of adjusting what they do. For instance: There are plenty of books and training programs out there that tell you that you *must* prospect for business in a certain way; typically, by picking up the phone and calling strangers so that you can ask them to meet with you in person. Now, some people are very, very good at this. It's called "cold calling." Other people, however—and John Hannah is one—have realized it's not the best use of their time, skill, and aptitudes. John has made the decision that he's better at prospecting for new business by meeting people face-to-face in social situations. *That's his right thing.* That's the kind of prospecting and business building that supports him professionally and that he has made a commitment to pursue at the level of excellence.

Giving other people right things to do that support organizational goals, by contrast, is an essential skill of entrepreneurs and effective managers.

What Questions Are You Asking?

The feedback you give people is what determines whether you are doing the right things or not doing the right things as an organization. Our feedback about

(Continued)

right things is based on questions we are constantly asking about what is happening in our stores. So: How do we work with our people in the stores? How do we communicate to them to look at what their activities are? How do we evaluate the actual tasks that they are engaged in to make sure they are doing the right things—the things that are going to be truly productive as opposed to the things that are just filling time and space?

—Paul Taylor

The fact that we are familiar with a certain activity is *not* in and of itself any proof that that activity constitutes one of the right things that supports our strategic intent. I may be familiar with the activity of catching up with friends, family, and professional acquaintances by hanging out on Facebook for three hours every day. If I analyze my time, however, I may reach the conclusion that my Facebook time does not actually get me any closer to any of my goals. By the same token, if something I'm used to doing connects with a strategic intent that the organization has completely abandoned, I may need to be coached into a new routine that's a little less familiar and a little more in line with what my team is trying to accomplish. Right things can and do change over time.

Evaluate . . . and Reevaluate!

In the interests of consistency, people tend to enact behaviors that may not actually be in their own best

(Continued)

(Continued)

interests—or in the best interests of the enterprise. So, we must constantly reevaluate what our people are actually doing, which is different from evaluating what we've told them to do, as far as "right things" are concerned. People tend to move back toward the "familiar things" instead, often even when a given "familiar thing" has been taken off their list of responsibilities.

—Kenneth Evans

DELEGATE THE RESPONSIBILITY—AND THE AUTHORITY!

When you delegate the responsibility to others in your organization, you have to be sure you delegate the authority, as well.

Are You Giving Your People a Shot at Success?

Some people are really fearful of being held accountable. It is scary for people to be told that they are accountable for something if they don't have the authority to make the desired result happen. So, if you are going to create a culture of accountability in your organization, you will also have to give the people the means—the resources—to get the job done. All right: You want to hold people accountable

(Continued)

---

for their results and their behavior. To get that, you have to give them a shot at their own success. You will have to ask them whether they really feel accountable; what they think accountability means; whether they can embrace that. The leader's ability to walk that talk, to make sure people get the tools and resources and *authority they need, can determine who's going to be a winner and who's going to be a loser in the organization.*

—Peter Aceto

One evening several years ago, when my oldest daughter, Sara, was in high school, I came into the computer room where she was doing her homework. Here's the picture I took in: She was sitting in front of the computer. Her notebook was on her right and her class book was on her left. Music was playing on the computer. Instant-message windows from her friends were popping up on the computer about every three seconds.

I didn't even know it was possible to hold 17 conversations simultaneously. It wears me out just thinking about it!

I couldn't help it. I went into parent mode. I said, "Sara, don't you think you could get done with your homework quicker if you finished your work first and *then* chatted with your friends?"

Sara looked back over her shoulder and sweetly asked, "Daddy, have you seen my grades lately?"

I knew what Sara's grades were, and she knew that I knew what her grades were. They were great. In fact, they were much better than mine were when I was in school. So, the only thing I could do was to gently tuck my tail between my legs, turn, and slowly slip out of the room.

You see, my wife, Renee, and I have given the responsibility to do well in school to our children. We have asked them to be accountable for doing the best they can. If their best is an A, great. If their best is a B, then so be it. We have also given them the authority to figure out *how* to do their best. If they slip below a B, then we step in. We delegate, but we don't abdicate.

It's our responsibility to check in and find out how our kids are doing. If you supervise people, it's the same with your team members. *Delegate both the responsibility and the authority* for your people to do the right things that support your organization—and then stay engaged enough to track whether they're actually delivering the results you and your team have agreed upon.

Only when you delegate both the responsibility and the accountability does the person feel that he or she owns the goal. And only when the person has that feeling of ownership is there going to be accountability.

Trust and Empowerment

The boss shows up and says, "Be responsible for this process." Then, the boss leaves. Do you feel more responsible than you did yesterday? Of course not.

What's missing? Well, you may be responsible for the outcome of this process, but you haven't been empowered to make changes to the process if that becomes necessary. You have to have both the responsibility and the authority. Otherwise, you can be told that you are responsible—you can be told that

(Continued)

you're accountable—but you won't really feel that way. Now, I, as the boss, may not be ready to give you that empowerment until I believe that you are going to make decisions that will be similar to the ones I would make. That's a question of trust. So, there is this relationship between trust and empowerment and accountability, and you really need to have all three of them. Otherwise, all you're doing is calling people accountable when they are not truly accountable. You haven't empowered them, because you don't trust them yet. You don't have that trust until they demonstrate some degree of accountability. So, you get this vicious cycle here. I believe there are two kinds of people in the world: the people who say, "You have to earn my trust," and the kind who say, "You know what? I hired you. That means I'm giving you the benefit of the doubt. You get to start out with my trust . . . but watch out, you can lose it." I prefer to take that leap of faith and allow people to start with trust, because you have to start somewhere. There is no real accountability without trust and empowerment.

—David Silverstein

KNOW YOUR OWN STRENGTHS AND WEAKNESSES

A leader must strive to be objective when answering the question, "What are my own right things?" This answer requires a commitment to be honest with oneself—and with the rest of the team—in identifying one's own aptitudes and skill gaps.

Park Your Ego Where You Park Your BMW

When it comes to being accountable to do the right things, self-awareness is key. Just look around—it's a trait the best leaders exhibit. They are especially self-aware—and while they most likely have strong egos, they are usually able to park those egos where they park their BMWs. That's what allows them to recognize their strengths and weaknesses. And the better leaders are transparent about this. You know, it's not a comfortable thing to talk to your direct reports or to other senior people and say, "Folks, here's where I'm really strong, and here is where I'm weak." Self-awareness can create clarity with your team on where your time will or will not be spent. It takes humility and a sense of trust in the team to be able to talk about these things. You have to see the discussion as a tool that enables your team to optimize the way you and they work together and thus more likely to accomplish greatness. You're not being critical. You're saying, "Hey, here's how we put all these different cylinders and all the pieces of the engine together, so we have a really fine-tuned engine."

—Jim McCool

ACCOUNTABILITY CHECK!

Now, it's time to expand your Accountability Zone.

Implement what you have learned about the first accountability.

Your primary accountability: Identify your strategic intent!

- What are you trying to accomplish and by when? Are you trying to generate the highest customer satisfaction levels for yachts manufactured in North America by two years from today? Lose 10 pounds within the next 90 days? Get your sales team 20 percent above quota this quarter?
- What activities—what right things—support that strategic intent?
- We are all accountable to someone! To whom will you be accountable (besides yourself) for identifying, evaluating, and implementing the right things that support your strategic intent? (The person you discuss these matters with may not be the person you're accountable to in terms of implementation.)

Individual focus: List five things that would have to happen for you to turn your strategic intent into a reality.

- When would you have to take action on them in order to make your schedule?
- What would have to happen today? What would have to happen every day?

- What are you doing right now that *does not* support

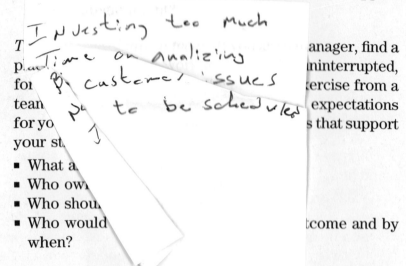

T[...] anager, find a
p[...] ninterrupted,
for [...] ercise from a
team [...] expectations
for yo[...] s that support
your st[...]

- What a[...]
- Who ow[...]
- Who shou[...]
- Who would [...] tcome and by
  when?

This is your first draft—think of it as a brainstorming document, an overview intended for your eyes only.

Do not publicize your list or formalize the accountabilities until you have completed the exercise at the conclusion of Chapter 6, "The Fourth Accountability: Establishing the Right Expectations."

For free tools that will help you implement this accountability, visit www.SamSilverstein.com.

THE SECOND ACCOUNTABILITY: MANAGING YOUR SPACE

Of the Five Accountabilities covered in this book, this is the one that my clients are most likely, at least at first, to think of as new or innovative. When you talk to successful people for long enough, however, what you find is that they have been holding themselves accountable on this score for years. They just did not have a name for what they were doing.

Adding by Subtracting

Most people think that when you take something away, when you truncate something, you are by definition less of a person, or less of a business, because you are abandoning what you were well known for doing before. I actually think that if you make the right decisions to reallocate your resources, you are

(Continued)

(*Continued*)

stronger, because you really know your focus, and you are choosing to focus on something that makes more sense. We are constantly managing our capacity—our mental, emotional, and economic capacity—to fulfill our mission in a sustainable way.

—Joan Magruder

We must be accountable to ourselves to create the new space we need to grow and innovate in our own lives, which sometimes means *taking* space from something else that we're doing. No one else is going to do that for us, and if we don't do it, it won't get done.

We are each accountable for asking the questions that allow us to manage our own space.

Would You Still Jump?

I have learned to ask a question that helps me to get out of that trap of continually doing the same thing over and over again. Forget about all the time and energy that you spent on it, whatever it is, and just ask yourself this question: If you had the exact same dollars today that you did back then, and knowing what you know now, would you jump into this opportunity or a different one? In our business, we created a logistics extension for overweight shipping. It was a major undertaking and a major investment—it gave us the ability to do a lot of things we hadn't done up to that point. But we decided

(*Continued*)

> to phase it out. We had to narrow the focus to stay profitable and to keep growing in our own space. We narrowed the focus and freed up a lot of resources and allowed us to do what we needed to do in our business.
>
> —Jeff Booth

A LESSON FROM A PLAID SPORTS COAT

A few years back, I was on a skiing trip with my family, and my daughters bought me this great North Face down jacket. I had seen it in a store and admired it, but I wasn't going to buy it. They surprised me with it and gave it to me as a gift! Of course, I loved the jacket, and I knew even before the trip was over that I would be wearing it a lot that winter.

When I returned home, I went to put the big down jacket into my hall closet where all my other coats were stored. Guess what? It wouldn't fit. There just wasn't enough space.

That's when I took a good, long look at all the coats I was keeping in that closet. I knew there were literally dozens of coats in there: coats I had not worn in years, coats I had only worn once, and even some coats I had sworn to myself I would never, ever wear again. There was a plaid jacket in there that must have dated back to the Carter administration.

I began to wonder something. Why hadn't I gotten rid of some of those coats—thrown them away or given them to charity—years ago? The answer was that I had simply gotten used to seeing them each time I opened that closet door. Now that I needed the space, I began to wonder how important the familiarity of that closet really was. There just wasn't enough space.

I started pulling out old jackets that I didn't wear any-more and putting them into a big pile to give to a local charity. The pile grew and grew. When I was done, my new down coat went in easily. I just had to clear out the old stuff so that I could make room for the new stuff, the stuff that really mattered to me: the new coat that I could now enjoy, that would improve my comfort level, and that would keep me warmer.

Exactly the same principle applies to our life and our business. We get so filled up with our familiar stuff, so used to seeing familiar stuff, and so used to navigating around familiar stuff that we forget to make the space for ourselves to try anything new. Force of habit prevents us from giving ourselves the physical, mental, financial, or emotional space necessary to shake things up a little bit and put something new in our lives—something that could provide growth and improvement.

Here's what I learned from a vintage 1979 plaid blazer: If mere force of habit is dictating our daily agenda, there is no room for anything new on that agenda, which means we are not managing our space efficiently or creating the space we need to pursue new opportunities for growth. We and we alone are accountable for making space for the new stuff by getting rid of the old stuff.

If we don't create space, we can't try new things. If we aren't trying new things, our competitors will beat us to new opportunities.

High achievers hold themselves accountable for making space for new growth. How do they do that? By managing their own space. They know they are personally responsi-ble for managing their own space, which means that they have to take the initiative to get new opportunities into the mix, even if that means getting rid of some familiar old opportunities. The fact that they're used to the old stuff doesn't make it a priority for them.

Your personal priorities must be based on your optimum choices, which are not necessarily your most familiar choices. Ask yourself: If you were all done making a living for the day by noon and you still had to do something productive, what would that something be? If you could do anything for that afternoon and you had the period from 1:00 P.M. to 6:00 P.M. absolutely open, what would you put in that slot? Once you know the answers to that question— whether they are "design a whole new product," or "reach out to my best customers," or "create a new market research initiative," or "build relationships with executives at other firms,"—ask yourself how you can work the best of those new initiatives into your schedule *tomorrow*. What will you get rid of to make space for the most important new priorities you've identified?

For instance: If you stopped handling all the phone prospecting yourself and delegated it to someone else who could do it just as well, what would you do with that time that could produce even greater results for you? If you're not willing to ask those (sometimes uncomfortable) questions, you're not managing your space effectively. You're using force of habit as a strategic forecasting tool. How much sense does that make?

Ask the Questions!

We redeployed a lot of our assets in the customer service area after asking ourselves, "How do our customers actually prefer to interact with us?"
(Continued)

> *(Continued)*
> What we found is that a lot of our customers were really more inclined to do things themselves than they were to ask for help. So, we were able to revise the budget and put the resources to work elsewhere, which we would never have done if we hadn't asked the question in the first place.
>
> —Pat Larmon

Suppose you were to decide that even though you've made money with a product or service in the past, you don't want to be married to it for the foreseeable future. What new products would you be able to fill your floor space with?

The choice to expand your business by getting rid of a profitable line and replacing it with something more relevant to your current goals may at first seem counterintuitive or even foolish. Yet, this is what great visionaries have always done. It's evidence of accountability and of your willingness to take seriously your responsibility to allocate your resources strategically.

Sometimes, accepting this responsibility means making dramatic changes in our lives and in our businesses. That is much better than pretending that whatever you're already doing always makes perfect strategic sense.

Eliminating 35 Percent of the Business

We chose more than a decade ago to eliminate any product that had anything to do with commissionable broker-dealer fees, because those products were
(Continued)

taking an inordinate amount of our time and were sending the wrong signals to our clients. We didn't see that it was in our best interest to continue offering them, so we got rid of them, even though they represented something like 35 percent of our business. This was a huge decision from a strategic standpoint and one of the best ones we've ever made. Over an 11-year period, that one decision led to 350 percent more revenue and was a big part of the reason we were able to grow faster than the market as a whole during that period.

—Peter Schick

APPLE DROPS THE MINI

A few years ago, Apple, the dominant player in the personal music player category, dropped its best-selling product, the iPod Mini. Why? Because they were launching a brand new product that took the iPod experience to another level: the iPod Nano. Most businesses would have been extremely hesitant to simply jettison a profitable product, let alone a category leader, regardless of what they had on the drawing board at the time. Apple was different. Why?

The answer: Apple's business philosophy was different. It was based on creating new space. The company's stated operating principle was—and is—that they would rather make themselves obsolete than watch the competition do it!

The iPod Mini represented where Apple had been. It was what everyone who was competing with Apple was trying to match. Apple's approach could have been to keep riding the same horse until it dropped. For a lot of companies, that strategy would have been seen as the safest. But Apple's senior management saw complacency as the bigger competitive danger.

Apple's senior management knew something that many business strategists forget: People and organizations usually cling to seemingly safe options for far too long out of sheer force of habit. When they do, they inevitably lose ground.

We are told as we are brought up, "A bird in the hand is worth two in the bush." I never hear anyone ask, "What if there are three birds in the bush? Or five? Or ten? How old is the bird in your hand, anyway? What if the bird that's in your hand is losing weight and isn't looking as chipper as it once did?" Assuming that you've got the right bird means that you're not managing your space.

We are accountable for managing our own space to create new possibilities for growth in income, pleasure, and personal development. We are accountable for moving beyond familiar patterns and finding new opportunities. "We've always done it that way" is, on its own, no excuse for not managing our space. Force of habit, though powerful, is no excuse for not managing our space. Familiarity, though comforting, is no excuse for not managing our space.

We are accountable to ask *what if.* We are responsible to explore where we can create space that could be filled with something that could offer us a greater yield.

Am I saying that all businesses should pick up their catalogs and cross out their number one product? Of course not. What I'm saying is that it may not make the most strategic sense for us to keep doing *everything* we're doing right now. I'm saying that we're responsible for acknowledging that something in our space could change. The question is, what is that something?

As Greg Joswiak, Apple's vice president of iPod and iPhone worldwide, put it: "Our competitors tend to put the cross-hairs on where we are now. By the time they come up with a product that tries to match where we are now, we're beyond them. We're one or two generations beyond, moving faster than they are."

Simplify, Simplify

Managing space is basically simplification. Lowe's went from offering 135,000 products to offering 93,000 products in their hardware stores. Sometimes, a simpler business is a more profitable business. So, what did they eliminate? Maybe they don't have 19 different types of lawn mowers on display anymore. Maybe people don't want to have every type of lawn mower to choose from. It almost becomes too much; people are overloaded, and they can't deal with all the technical specifications they have to analyze in order to make a good choice. Maybe Lowe's listened to the consumer who said, "Look, all I want is a lawn mower to mow the grass. I don't need to have four different kinds of hedgers to choose from, each with twelve different attachments."

—Michael Staenberg

A NEW WINDOW OF OPPORTUNITY

Back in the 1970s, my father-in-law, an immigrant who had lived through the horrors of the Dachau concentration camp during World War II, started a company called Delsan

Aluminum Industries. The company's main product was aluminum storm windows.

The firm did very well. Indeed, my father-in-law pretty much lived the American dream during the company's early years. It grew so fast, in fact, that my father-in-law decided he needed some help.

By the time my brother-in-law and I decided to buy into the company in the early 1980s, Delsan was enjoying some pretty remarkable success in the marketplace. In fact, we were a major provider of aluminum storm windows in the Midwest.

Then something astonishing happened: We found a whole new market.

Shortly before I joined Delsan, my father-in-law had introduced a new product line: vinyl replacement windows. I vowed to push the volume on the new window products, and push it I did. The sales exceeded everyone's expectations and just kept growing.

The new offering transformed our business. We were accumulating huge numbers of new accounts—accounts that were worth more, far more, than the average customer that had made my father-in-law a wealthy man. I realized that we were capable of doing things in the marketplace with vinyl products that we'd never been able to do before with the aluminum ones. We started looking for new vinyl products to pull into the mix, and the response got even better.

This presented us with an interesting situation. The aluminum storm window had established us as a company and was an "emotional favorite" for us. We thought of it as the heart of the company. It was making money. But it was not our core product anymore, and its volume was dropping.

We realized that we had to take a long, hard look at the direction of our business.

We did an analysis and concluded that we were not turning our inventory fast enough on the aluminum products to justify continuing their presence in our line. That hurt, but it was true. Another problem was that the floor space required to manufacture the aluminum windows was massive; we could use the same space to create vinyl products and generate at least four or five times the product volume (and by extension, four or five times the profit) from the same space. What was more, we had a lot of new vinyl product lines that we wanted to add and currently couldn't.

We changed our name to Delsan Industries, and we sold off our signature product—the genesis of the entire organization, the aluminum storm window. This product had made the company millions of dollars in years past and was still profitable. But it was the wrong investment for us as an organization.

We needed new space.

Selling off the old line was a hard decision, but it was a very sound move strategically, because it allowed us to focus on the products that would take our company to the next level. If we had decided to simply continue making aluminum storm windows because that was what we were familiar with doing and good at doing, we would have followed a very different path in the years ahead.

I liked the path we chose. It led us to exponential growth and a level of commercial success that we could hardly have imagined before we took on the vinyl line. We sold off Delsan Industries to a Fortune 500 company just a few years after we eliminated the aluminum products that previously had been at the core of our business.

This one business decision not only bought us the physical space we needed to expand our business, but it also established an important decision-making and leadership precedent for the next phase of our business's growth. It generated *leadership* space.

With this move, we confirmed something essential about our organization and the way we were going to take it where it had to go next. We made it clear to everyone in the organization that what we were familiar with or successful at doing in the past was always open for review. Of course, not every company feels that way about its core business lines.

But that wasn't all. With this decision, we also made it clear that the company leadership was *responsible* for launching new ideas and new initiatives. That was true, even if it meant leaving behind something that made a lot of emotional sense or something that was still working for us. We confirmed, as a working principle, that *creating* new opportunities, creating new space, was part of our job description as company leaders and part of what we expected from others in the organization. We had to create space to try new things and grow. That was now part of our culture.

By the way, we sold the aluminum storm window business to the plant manager who had been operating it for years. By setting him up in his own business, we took care of a loyal employee who had been with us a long time, and in doing so, we also made space on the management team for someone whose skills were more relevant to the market we now faced. We still needed products from the former plant manager, and in fact, we became one of his major customers. Several years later, he sold the business and retired on its proceeds.

No Sacred Cows

I spend most of my time these days on the subject of innovation, and I think perhaps one of the biggest obstacles to innovation is the fear of cannibalizing your own business. That's not always a bad thing. You have to be willing to kill things and also to cannibalize your own business in order to grow. You have to understand what all those sacred cows are, and you have to ask yourself whether they are so sacred after all. A new idea may just justify getting rid of one of those cows.

—David Silverstein

"DISNEY'S FOLLY"

Walt Disney was the king of the short cartoon in the mid-1930s, and he was making plenty of money in the middle of the Great Depression, but he didn't want to *keep on* being the king of the short cartoon. He wanted to master a new form, and he wanted to grow his business at an even faster rate. So, Walt went beyond what was safe, what was familiar, and what was predictable, and he turned his business upside down. He invested everything he had, and then some, in a new venture: a full-length animated feature.

No one had made money with a full-length animated feature before, and there were plenty of people who thought Walt was a fool to bet his entire studio on such an undertaking. Some people believed that audiences would be overwhelmed by the visual stimulation of an

79

80-minute cartoon and would walk out on the feature halfway through, no matter the quality of the film. Others couldn't imagine a full-length "gag film," which was what they imagined the Disney studio was making: a very, very long Mickey Mouse cartoon. The film industry know-it-alls dismissed the project as "Disney's Folly," and Disney's own wife advised him that no one would pay a dime to see this picture.

Walt thought otherwise and went about reinventing his own studio. Every available resource was channeled toward the new project.

He knew full well that the technology did not exist to make the animated movie he had in mind. He wanted the depth of field and the three-dimensional feeling of a well-made live-action film. Instead of relying on the same tools that had made him a household name with his Mickey Mouse and Three Little Pigs shorts, he resolved to create the new tools he and his team would need. *He made new space for himself.* That new space was called *Snow White and the Seven Dwarfs.*

The technical advances necessary to bring *Snow White and the Seven Dwarfs* out of Disney's head and onto the screen had to be built from scratch. They included a revolutionary multiplate shooting system that gave what was (and remains) an astonishing illusion of depth and movement in many of the shots, an effect designed to pull viewers instantly into the world of the picture. He also resolved to make the characters lifelike by shooting many of the scenes based on live-action footage that was pains-takingly retraced, frame by frame, to create some of the characters—notably, Snow White herself.

No one had ever combined those elements into an animated film before, and no one had spent the kind of money on an animated picture that Disney was spending. The rumors of the project's ever-escalating expenses astonished some and delighted others who were eager to see Walt Disney fail. And for a while, it looked to many people that he would fail. The fact is, he ran out of money long before he ran out of movie.

Disney's quest for new space was backed by commitment and definiteness of purpose and can serve, even in our era of $100 million and up movie budgets, as a reminder of how important it is to stay resolved and focused on your goal. Once you've charted a new path and set aside something that works to make an investment in something that you know could work even better, you must stay the course. And that's what Walt Disney did. Having already spent every penny his company had, and having mortgaged his own home and put every cent of that into *Snow White*, Walt Disney had only half a movie. He needed another $1 million to complete the project. And he needed it at a time when most of the experts in the movie industry were convinced that he was out of his mind and when about a third of the American labor force was out of work. Times were hard, money was tight, and the buzz around the movie was not good. No one would have been surprised if Disney had walked away from the task of reinventing himself, his studio, and the motion picture industry.

But he didn't walk away. He put together a screening of the film using the footage that he did have, some of which was rough and only black and white, for a senior lender at Bank of America. And he got his $1 million.

He created the new space he knew his company needed to take on this new task; he finished the picture and released the first great animated feature film in movie history. At the time of its first release, *Snow White and the Seven Dwarfs* quickly became the most successful motion picture of all time. (It would retain that ranking for two years, until the release of *Gone with the Wind.*)

All of what happened from that point forward at Disney's company—all the animated breakthroughs, all the great characters, all the merchandising, all the theme parks, all the television ventures—would not have occurred if Disney had not decided to leave behind what was familiar and create new space for himself and his organization. He *believed* in the space to do something new that he was creating for himself and his company.

What new space will *you* create for yourself? What new direction makes the most sense for you? Will you believe in it as deeply and with as much commitment as Disney brought to *his* new direction?

A Lesson from a Master

I was at a point in my career where I was frustrated and questioning whether I was able to play basketball at the NBA level. Then, I ran into Wilt Chamberlain one day while I was working out. He had been watching me. He pointed to the lane in front of the basket and said, "This is what you can be great at. Guard this basket. Own the key. Keep people away from the basket. You're seven-foot-four; you don't have to race up and down the court with the shorter and faster players." In that five-minute conversation, Wilt showed me how to manage my space. I was able to set the single-season record for blocked shots,

(Continued)

> make the All-Star team, and do a whole lot of other things in the NBA, but it really all started with that five-minute conversation with Wilt. He brought it home for me. You have to know what you can be great at. You need to know what to let go of, so you can figure out what you should be focusing on.
>
> —Mark Eaton

ACCOUNTABILITY CHECK!

Now, it's time to expand your Accountability Zone.

Implement what you have learned about the second accountability.

Your primary accountability check: Manage your space! Answer each of the following questions in writing with at least two full sentences.

- Imagine your day now has 36 hours, and imagine you have an unlimited budget. If time were not an issue, if resources were not an issue, and if physical space were not an issue, what would you do in addition to what you're doing right now?
- What new priorities would you take on?

- What would you have to change in order to make that happen?
- What would you have to eliminate?
- *We are all accountable to someone!* To whom will you be accountable (besides yourself) for evaluating new opportunities to manage your space in the future?

Individual focus: What new initiatives could you pursue tomorrow to support your strategic intent that you didn't do today? Make a written list. Create at least three possibilities.

Team or organization focus: As a manager, answer each of the following questions in depth.

- If you were building this team, this department, or this organization from scratch *today*—knowing what you know now—what would you do differently?
- What differences would there be in terms of your investments of time and resources?
- What differences would there be in terms of staffing?
- What projects would you eliminate?
- What priorities would you change?
- What new projects would you take on and why?

5

THE THIRD ACCOUNTABILITY:
MANAGING THE PROCESS

*O*nce upon a time, a father needed to buy his daughter a pair of soccer shoes after her old pair of soccer shoes fell apart during a late-afternoon game. This was the day before her big game, which was to take place first thing the next morning. The father checked his watch and realized that he had about 15 minutes left before the store's closing time. Unfortunately, he was about a 25-minute drive from the store, even if he pushed the speed limit. Should he

(a) give up and tell his daughter she was just going to have to play the game in tennis shoes?
(b) pray for a rainout?
(c) give his daughter some money and tell her to solve the problem herself?
(d) get in his car, pull out his cell phone, call up the store manager, and negotiate 10 extra minutes so that

he could buy the shoes his daughter needed for her game?

If you picked option (d) —as I did, being the father in question—you already have a head start on mastering the third accountability.

Managing the process is what happens when our strategic intent faces an obstacle, and we still move forward to take creative action toward attaining the goal.

This is being personally accountable for making progress toward whatever it is we are trying to make happen. This is not giving up the minute we face some situation or challenge that doesn't support our goal. This is not throwing up our hands and saying, "If it's not meant to be, it's not meant to be."

This is accepting proactive accountability for *making* it happen.

How Will You React to Change?

The real problem with the way that some people look at accountability is that oftentimes it's layered into a notion of a rigid set of expectations and performance parameters, and frankly, you can get into very deep trouble if that's your mantra. How you react to changing events is important as well.

—Kenneth Evans

BEYOND "WE TRIED"!

If you've spent any time as a manager, I think you know exactly what skill I'm talking about here.

Here's my question for the managers who are reading this book: Have you ever had the experience of delegating the responsibility for something important and then having the person you delegated it to drop the ball the moment some new and unfamiliar situation or problem presented itself?

The person didn't navigate a new path forward based on the new situation, didn't come close to the best obtainable outcome, didn't come to you and ask for help or guidance in navigating the difficulty, and didn't even tell you that he or she stopped trying to make progress toward the goal! That action item you delegated simply fell off the edge of the earth, and you actually had to *remind* the person that you had delegated that task to him or her. Once you did, you heard an excuse: "*We tried*, but such and such happened. I wasn't sure what to do."

If you've ever had that experience as a manager, then you know what managing the process is. It's what you wished that person had done for you *instead* of dropping the ball. It's moving beyond "We tried"!

Effective people and effective organizations accept full accountability for managing the process rather than let unforeseen obstacles and unanticipated events manage them. We don't stop being accountable for delivering on our strategic intent when we hit a bump in the road. We accept personal responsibility for negotiating the best possible outcome based on whatever circumstances actually arise.

Stay in Accountability!

At the end of the day, we have to be agile enough to recognize when things are not going well and to
(Continued)

(Continued)

identify different courses of action, as long as they are legitimate and fair and honest, and then start to manage those processes. One of the things that we are looking at in our own organization is that it is very difficult to predict with any great degree of accuracy how our business is going to perform from quarter to quarter. Now, on one hand, we could say, "Okay, well, we can't control it." That would take us out of accountability.

What I constantly preach instead to my direct reports is how important it is for us to do two things. First, we have to be willing to step up as soon as we anticipate that we are going to have a problem, and we have to be open and transparent about that, because bad news does not get better with age. And then second, we have to identify the things we can do to mitigate the problem. If we think we are going to fall short of our revenue projections, is there anything we can do from a cost standpoint to improve the situation? If we just wait until the end of the quarter, it will be too late to go back and make any of those adjustments.

—Richard Chambers

WHAT WILL YOU DO?

In the real world, you are going to encounter unwelcome developments on your way to the attainment of any worthy goal. What will you do when that happens?

Whenever you do run into adversity (and you will), your response to it will confirm for yourself, and everyone else, exactly what kind of person you are: someone who is personally accountable for managing the process or someone who isn't.

Being *personally* accountable for managing the process is a trait of Highly Accountable People. Let me ask you this: How many people do you really, truly admire who duck responsibility when things get tough? If you take a moment to think of the truly successful people you've met (or even heard about) in your own life, you'll probably realize that each of them was willing to accept responsibility for managing the process. If you're interested in learning how to *become* one of those people, read on.

Good Leaders, Poor Leaders

Every day we are faced with situations that are unexpected and are not within our control. One of the other things that distinguishes a good leader from a poor one is the ability to understand how to cope with and adjust to such situations.

—Sir Andrew Likierman

"WHICH PAINTING IS YOUR FAVORITE?"

Several years ago, my wife, Renee, and I spent a few days in Santa Fe, New Mexico. Just up from the city center is a wonderful area called Canyon Road; it's about a mile long, and it's lined with artists' galleries on both sides. Renee and I walked in and out of the various galleries as we strolled down the street. We had *no intention of buying a painting*. In fact, I didn't particularly want to buy anything that afternoon.

Renee and I came across one gallery featuring Phyllis Kapp, a prominent local artist. After we walked through all of the rooms, admiring the magnificent paintings, we saw a well-dressed lady approaching us. It turned out that Phyllis herself was in the gallery that day.

She started a conversation; we began chatting pleasantly with her. Eventually, Phyllis asked, "Which painting is your favorite?"

The moment those words were out of her mouth, I remember thinking to myself, *She's managing the process!* After all, we had no intention of buying a painting or anything else. Phyllis had the strategic intent of selling a painting, and we'd given her no indication whatsoever that we wanted to buy anything. She was in a situation where her strategic intent faced an obstacle (our silence). By asking that question, she was taking action toward her goal, anyway.

We still had no intention to buy a painting, but more out of a sense of courtesy than anything else, we took Phyllis back into one of the rooms and pointed out a particular piece that was hanging in the middle of the wall. It was a watercolor with bright, vibrant colors: a desert landscape with mountains and a beautiful sky. "That's our favorite," my wife said. (She was right, of course; before Phyllis had shown up, we'd each mentioned that we'd liked that painting.)

Phyllis proceeded to tell us all about that particular piece. She told us how she had come to paint it, what she was trying to accomplish with the piece, what other work had influenced her, and so on. Then, she asked us another great question: "Where in your house do you imagine this hanging?"

Phyllis was still managing the process. Think about what has to happen in order for that piece of art to hang in our house. Of course: We would have to buy it. *She was asking us a question whose very answer required us to buy the picture—in our minds.* And getting us to buy the painting was, of course, Phyllis's strategic intent.

We hadn't walked in the door looking for a painting to buy, but when Phyllis asked that question, we actually started thinking about where it might look best in our home.

I smiled and answered, "In our family room."

And that's where the painting is hanging today.

Was this some kind of magic trick? Did her question *always* get people to start thinking about where they'd hang her work? Of course not. Nothing sells paintings—or produces any other positive outcome—100percent of the time. I'm confident, however, that Phyllis does sell a lot more paintings than a person who never manages the process. Phyllis was (and is) the kind of person who routinely takes proactive responsibility for moving things forward *as far as she can* in support of her strategic intent.

Are you?

Defiantly Adjust to the Situation

Shortly after I arrived at NYU Medical Center, I lost two of my best surgeons. One of them decided to leave to take another position, and the other one,

(Continued)

(Continued)

unfortunately, passed away suddenly. It was quite a situation to walk into! Even though everyone was panicking, and some people even said that we had to close all operations, I looked at it as an opportunity to upgrade our services and upgrade our capabilities. On very short notice, we were able to recruit one of the top surgeons in the country. So, we defiantly adjusted ourselves to a situation that we were not able to control. What we could control was our recruitment effort. We enlisted the help of the entire administration, from the dean down to the chair of surgery, and the result was that we found one of the best surgeons in the country.

—Achi Ludomirsky

ARE YOU MANAGING THE PROCESS OR ABDICATING IT?

At any given moment, you are either managing the process or abdicating. Any time you abdicate, any time you stop making an effort to adjust to whatever obstacle you've encountered and pursue your strategic intent, you've stepped out of your Accountability Zone. Many people, as you've probably noticed, are very good at abdicating and spend *most* of their time and energy explaining why they *can't* move forward on a goal. The same energy that could go into creating a new pathway to the goal instead goes into explanations and excuses and stories about all the terrible things the world has done to keep us from being able to move forward. We can't always control what happens in this world, but we can control the choices we make in response to whatever does happen.

Phyllis didn't let fate or luck determine her outcome. She took action and managed the process.

In stark contrast, most of the galleries that we went into did not manage the process. Instead, they abdicated!

Here's what abdicating looks like: Some of the galleries we looked at that day simply let people walk in and walk out, without ever engaging them in conversation. Most of the galleries we visited were overseen by someone who wasn't very good at establishing rapport. Typically, that person walked up to us and asked what you and I have been asked hundreds of times before in hundreds of stores: "May I help you?" That person wasn't managing the process. He or she was reciting a question that could, and did, routinely receive responses that pushed the conversation *further away* from the strategic intent of selling a painting.

When I said what so many of us would say—"No thanks, I'm just looking"—the person said, "Okay, let me know if you need any help," and the conversation ended. You could tell that some of these people really didn't want to be having the conversation at all. In fact, I think they were *terrified* of having the conversation in the first place! They were not willing to be accountable for managing the process. That's a shame, because *the lower your accountability for managing the process, the less effective you will be at negotiating outcomes that support your strategic intent.*

Managing the process takes practice, just like any other worthy undertaking in life. The more practice you give yourself, the more comfortable you will be when it comes time to take action that supports your strategic intent. You can always tell which person in a given situation is effectively managing the process. It's the person who isn't terrified of improvising.

People who are used to improvising when they encounter an obstacle to their strategic intent have learned to think on their own feet. They're comfortable doing so, just like Phyllis was. They've learned to *keep moving forward toward the goal*—even though there's no instruction book around to tell them exactly what has to happen next.

Phyllis got an A in my book, because she created her own Accountability Zone. She knew that *she and she alone* was accountable for managing the process. Someone across the street who says "May I help you?" and "Let me know if you need anything" gets an F!

If you are not accountable to manage the process, you have left the Accountability Zone. You are ceding accountability for some aspect of your life to forces outside of your control.

EXAMINE NEAR MISSES!

Managing the process, as we've seen, is what we do when we encounter an obstacle, and we still find some way to make headway on our strategic intent. One big asset in managing the process is close analysis of the phenomenon known as a *near miss*. A near miss in the world of air traffic control is what happens when a pilot *almost* encounters a major obstacle—namely, another aircraft. That encounter could have derailed the pilot's strategic intent of completing the journey safely, but thanks to quick thinking on the pilot's part, the mission is not compromised.

The near miss idea applies not only to processes that affect human safety but to every undertaking with the potential to affect our strategic intent. That means we want to know about the sales that were *nearly* lost, the defective units that were *nearly* shipped, the P.R. disaster that *nearly* played out.

These are important events. The government mandates that airlines maintain full accountability for reporting, categorizing, and analyzing their near misses, so they'll be more effective at managing the process when similar circumstances arise in the future. We must hold ourselves accountable for the same kind of close analysis. Just thanking our lucky stars that we didn't crash is not enough! *The more we learn about our own near misses in any given area, the better we and our organization will be at managing the process in that area.*

This is one of the areas that Highly Accountable People are endlessly committed to. They never stop asking these great questions: "What do our near misses teach us? What have we learned? How can we keep this problem from arising again?"

Don't ask me why this kind of event is called a near miss rather than a near hit; that's one of those inscrutable mysteries of life. The point is, a responsible review of any project must include an above-board discussion and analysis of *all* the near misses that we've experienced. We can't wait for a plane to crash before we conduct a review of whether our airline's safety procedures are appropriate! We have to look closely at the accidents that *almost* happened, the collisions that were *narrowly* averted, and the people who were *nearly* hurt and adjust accordingly.

If we are truly accountable, we will recognize these events for the blessings in disguise that they are. *Near misses tell us where there are likely to be challenges that keep us from realizing our strategic intent.*

Warning: Leaders within any process-focused organization must go out of their way to *praise and reward* individuals who report near misses. If your company culture rewards the opposite behavior—concealing near misses—or punishes people who try to call attention to near misses, *you will not have the information you need to improve your organization over time.* It is impossible to create a truly accountable organization without rewarding the people who help you learn from near misses and manage the process based on what you've learned.

THE ULTIMATE LIFE SKILL?

Learning to manage the process may be the ultimate life skill. This skill affects *everything.* Let's say you're at the airport, and your flight is cancelled. You can either go get in line like all of the other people who are willing to wait for the agent to book them on another flight, or you can manage the process. For my own part, when I encounter this situation, I don't make a habit of standing in line as though I were a bewildered, obedient sheep. I pull out my cell phone, I call the airline's phone reservation line, and within a matter of minutes, I have a seat on the next available flight. I'm off down the concourse. I've noticed that sometimes when my new flight is getting ready to take off, there are still people in that long line, waiting to be taken care of. *That's managing the process in action!*

We can't always get what we want. But we can always manage the process, and we can always see just how close we can come to getting what we really want.

Aren't you curious? How close can you get to what you really want?

Are You Managing the Process?

A while ago, when Wall Street sort of collapsed, virtually every hospital found itself facing major shortfalls in terms of its investment income—which is a major source of capital for hospitals. Overnight, most hospitals were looking at portfolios that had dropped by 30 percent or more. And so, the question is, how do you respond to that? About 90 percent of our competitors responded by simply freezing capital projects, discontinuing benefits, cutting tuition, and so on. Instead of doing that, we said, "Wait a minute—most hospitals are not-for-profit organizations; they don't live quarter by quarter. Our mission is not to deliver a dividend to investors."

We decided to send the message, internally and externally, that it was important for people's care that we keep building private beds, keep investing in cutting-edge technology, keep managing infection control. So, for me, managing the process meant accepting that yes, we will have some cash depletion in the short term and we will have to be smart, but our investment income will come back. In the meantime, we are going to stick to our priorities. Why was something we thought was very important a year ago suddenly not important? Instead of accepting that kind of thinking, we have put a lot more energy into looking for waste, into lean initiative. Unlike our competitors, we have stayed the course when it comes to reinvesting in the things that we consider most important to our mission for the medium term and

(Continued)

> (*Continued*)
>
> long term. We're not going to overreact because of a short-term change.
>
> —*Joan Magruder*

Suppose the news reports tell us that the economy is struggling. Do we let someone else's assessment of what the economy is or isn't doing determine what we will do next in our lives, or do we assume accountability for managing the process ourselves?

Does the bad economy really run our choices about how we're going to do our job, how we're going to respond to opportunities we find, and how we're going to deal with the inevitable obstacles we will encounter along the way to success? Is the bad economy accountable for determining what happens next in our lives, or are we?

A sales manager I know of was debriefing with one of his salespeople following a meeting with a hot prospect—a company that represented potentially millions of dollars in business. The sales manager asked the salesperson what had happened during the meeting, and the salesperson answered, "Well, it turns out they're not buying."

The sales manager asked, "Why not?"

And the salesperson replied, "Let's face it: We're in a tough economy. That's the reality we're up against now."

Wrong answer. The sales manager hit the roof. He said, "The *economy* is why you didn't close the sale? Don't tell me that. Tell me you didn't close the sale because of something *you* could have done differently or *I* could have done differently or the *company* could have done differently, so we can figure out how to do it better the next time. But don't tell me it's the *economy's* fault that you didn't get this commission, because I won't believe you. If you'd *closed* the deal, would you want me to give 20 percent of the sale to *the economy* instead of putting it on your paycheck?"

When you hit an obstacle, you are the one who is accountable for finding a way forward. It's not the economy. It's not the president. It's not your first-grade teacher who made fun of you years ago. It's you.

I think we're all tempted at times to abdicate in just the way that salesperson did—to step away from managing the process and buy into excuses. *Every time we make an excuse and every time we abdicate, we stop managing the process.* And when that happens, we move out of the Accountability Zone.

"WHAT CAN I DO TO RAISE MY GRADE?"

Managing the process is something we are accountable for in all walks of life and in all disciplines. We get dozens, maybe hundreds of opportunities to manage the process each and every day.

My daughter Jackie calculated after a big test that she was right on the bubble in a college class she was taking. If her grade was rounded down, she would get a B. If it was rounded up, she would get an A. *She wanted the A. That was her strategic intent.*

Instead of doing nothing, instead of complaining about the situation, and instead of saying "If it's not meant to be, it's not meant to be," she assumed personal accountability for attaining her outcome. She scheduled a meeting with the teacher, shared how hard she had been working in the class, and asked if there was any extra-credit assignment she could do to push her grade over the hump from B to A. The teacher, impressed with her initiative, gave her an extra-credit task; she completed it, and she overcame the obstacle, thus fulfilling her strategic intent.

Jackie managed the process.

HOUSTON, ARE WE ACCOUNTABLE?

Have you seen the film *Apollo 13* about the real-life NASA mission that sustained an unexpected explosion en route to the moon? The blast disabled the spacecraft, threatened the lives of its three crew members, and left Mission Control with a brand new strategic intent: that of getting three astronauts home safely in a crippled ship. Can you imagine how differently that movie would have ended if the lead participants in the drama had stopped managing the process and started making excuses instead?

Astronaut: "Houston, we've got a problem."

Mission Control: "Copy that. We want you to know that whatever the problem is, Apollo, it wasn't Mission Control's fault. This is an issue that arose because our vendors let us down, our budgets have been slashed, and the weather is really lousy outside today, which has a lot of the people here facing some serious morale problems. We have no record of a problem at this point in time on any of the simulations that took place. Last but not least, we haven't really budgeted for a problem here, so we'd appreciate you referring to this with some other term, such as 'incident' or 'event,' for accounting purposes. Good luck sorting this out, whatever it is. If there's anything you want the public relations people to pass along, please feel free to leave us a message."

That's abdicating—the *opposite* of managing the process. Here's what managing the process sounded like in the film (and, I suspect, in real life):

NASA director: "This could be the worst disaster NASA's ever faced."

Flight Chief Gene Kranz: "With all due respect, sir, I believe this is gonna be our finest hour."

Let's think for a moment about what actually happened on Apollo 13. The mission was to be the third manned landing on the moon, and it was launched at a point when a moon landing was seen by some members of the public as routine. *Routine* means that there's no adversity, no obstacle, no problem to overcome. You're following the plan, and it's working. There are no bumps in the road.

No space mission is actually routine, of course. There are countless adversities and challenges to deal with as any such mission moves forward. Everyone at NASA knew that much. But the world at large figured out for sure that the Apollo 13 mission *really* wasn't routine when word came that one of the ship's oxygen tanks had blown up, causing another tank to fail, crippling the command module, and forcing the crew to move into the lunar module, which became their lifeboat.

Suddenly, the moon no longer mattered. There was a new strategic intent: getting the crew home safely, despite the many obstacles that appeared to stand in the way of that goal. A new course had to be plotted for earth. With navigational systems down, the astronauts would have to manually reorient the ship for a safe trajectory back to earth, using the sun as a navigational point. The lunar module, where the men were now camping out, was close to freezing. There was limited oxygen and even less water—barely enough water to sustain life and cool the ship during final phases of the trip home. The oxygen filters in the lunar module had been designed for two men, not three. This meant that with every breath, the astronauts were taxing the system and coming closer to poisoning themselves with carbon monoxide. The astronauts would have to create new filters from scratch to fit the lunar module's system. Last but not least, the power situation was critical: If the crew did not find some way to use its available power more efficiently, they would die before they reached earth.

None of these problems had clear solutions at the time they arose. All of them demanded the capacity to manage the process creatively, persistently, and collaboratively.

Procedures for the new mission had to be created from scratch—and tested on the ground in Houston— more or less instantly. There were no protocols for handling the new and daunting series of obstacles that had arisen. Working together, the astronauts and Houston had to assume *mutual* accountability for managing the process and for moving forward toward the goal, *despite* a lack of experience in resolving the obstacles that had presented themselves. I'll be sharing more thoughts on the important subject of mutual accountability in the next chapter, "The Fourth Accountability: Establishing the Right Expectations."

If people had tried to follow an existing script, if they had used the old job descriptions, or if they had wasted time figuring out whose fault it was that the tanks had exploded, the new strategic intent of saving the men from disaster would have been compromised, and the astronauts would almost certainly not have made it home. As it happened, the team as a whole, in space and on the ground, was able to work together to manage the process.

When the lives of the Apollo 13 astronauts were in grave and immediate danger, NASA didn't throw up its collective hands and say, "Well, I guess a successful outcome to this mission just wasn't meant to be." Why are so many people ready to relinquish their accountability for managing the process when they hit obstacles that are far less daunting?

"Failure Is Not an Option"

Gene Kranz, the mission control director for Apollo 13, had a saying: "Failure is not an option." As businesses are beset with setbacks and failures, likewise, individuals suffer setbacks and failures—but in spite of those risks, we should set lofty goals. We should have an expectation that We—and that is with a capital "W"—can solve the most intractable or seemingly impossible situations. That mindset has to become part of the culture. There's a sense of undying optimism that I think is a characteristic of many great leaders; a sense that somehow, we will figure this out. Apollo 13 is my favorite example of inspiring leadership against near impossible circumstances.

—Jim McCool

To provide that kind of leadership, we must model the skill of thinking and acting creatively. Following the most familiar set of instructions wouldn't have gotten the Apollo 13 astronauts home safely, and it won't get your team past the many unpredictable challenges they will encounter.

Change Your Angle

We get companies face-to-face appointments with C-level decision makers at major firms. Sometimes, I've left a decision maker over a hundred voice-mail messages before I booked an appointment with that person, but I didn't leave the *same* voice-mail message, and I didn't *stop* leaving messages. Whenever you hit a roadblock and there's a big boulder in your way, you have to change your angle if you want to find the "sweet spot" that will crack the boulder in two.

—Christine Aquin

ACCOUNTABILITY CHECK!

Now, it's time to expand your Accountability Zone.

Implement what you have learned about the third accountability.

Your primary accountability check: Identify opportunities to manage the process! Answer each of the following questions in writing with at least two full sentences.

- What is the biggest obstacle you are currently facing in turning your strategic intent into reality?

- How have you typically dealt with that obstacle in the past—by managing the process or by abdicating?
- How could you manage the process in dealing with these obstacles in the future?
- *We are all accountable to someone*! To whom will you be accountable (besides yourself) for managing the process on this issue in the future?

Individual focus: What is the biggest obstacle standing in the way of you attaining your personal strategic intent right now?

- How will you manage the process in dealing with that obstacle *tomorrow*?

Team or organization focus: As a manager, answer each of the following questions in depth.

- Within each of the major functional areas of your business—sales, manufacturing, operations, human resources, and so forth—list one problem you have faced consistently and so far haven't been able to overcome.
- Working with your team, identify three or four ways to manage the process in dealing with each of those situations.
- What near misses have occurred in each of these functional areas? Ask your team to provide examples, and then discuss those examples in depth.
- What risks would you and your organization face if one of those near misses turned into an actual crisis?
- What steps can you take today to minimize your exposure to those risks?

6

THE FOURTH ACCOUNTABILITY: ESTABLISHING THE RIGHT EXPECTATIONS

Expectations are the targets we set for ourselves. Once we accept them, they determine our actions, our outlook, and our destinies. They create our world. Expectations are worth setting consciously. But we often set them heedlessly, both for ourselves and for others.

Make the Goal Obtainable

Sometimes, the goals are set too high. A goal that people believe is not obtainable is not motivating, because it is not real. You can't visualize it. You have no evidence for it, no benchmarks that support

(Continued)

(Continued)
it. The other challenge comes when the bar is set so low that you trip over it. I think one of the worst things you can do to someone is refuse to stretch them. All of us need to come up against a little resistance in life. So, there's an art to setting our own expectations, and by the same token, there's an art to setting expectations for other people. Each individual person we work with needs to have a unique goal that the person perceives as realistic and that at the same time stretches that person a little.

—Brian Martin

Expectations are our view of what is attainable and what is possible. We are accountable for establishing not just any expectation but the *right* expectation, both for ourselves as individuals and for the team we oversee.

The fourth accountability is all about figuring out what the potential is in a given situation and then adjusting our expectations accordingly, in alignment with our strategic intent. The quality of our expectations inevitably determines the quality of our measurable results, both individually and organizationally.

We are accountable for *what* we decide to expect from ourselves, *how* we decide to strive for it, and whether we actually *measure* the outcomes of our efforts to fulfill those expectations. *Managing our expectations on an ongoing basis is essential.* Our quality of life depends in large degree on our ability to manage expectations.

When we allow ourselves simply to base our expectations on past results, we are not effectively managing our expectations. *The present and the future may have entirely different requirements than those we faced in the past, and our own capacities may be far greater than we realize.*

Get the Expectations Right

I don't think it is possible to overstate how important it is to get the expectations set properly in the beginning, regardless of what it is you are talking about. If you can't set reasonable expectations for yourself and others, everything else is for naught.

—George Tamke

We all have expectations, but not all of us accept accountability for establishing the *right* expectations for the situation we face and managing them on an ongoing basis. The following story will make the distinction clear.

THE $5,000 MAN

Back in 1960, Maxwell Maltz wrote a remarkable book called *Psycho-Cybernetics*. It's a book about our accountability to manage our own expectations.

Cybernetics is a real-life science, the science of goal-driven systems—guided missiles, for instance, that can hit a moving target in midair, or a piece of computer software that identifies the shortest route from point A to point B. These are systems that are designed to attain a certain goal. Maltz's book proposes that the human brain and nervous system are themselves cybernetic systems. He argues that human beings live *goal-focused* lives. The problem is, they don't always realize what goals they've set for themselves and sometimes don't even choose those goals consciously.

One example Maltz gives is of a salesperson working in the 1950s who managed to make $5,000 in a single year from a subpar sales territory. Even back then, $5,000 a year wasn't a huge amount of money, but it was a high enough figure to make this salesperson's manager wonder what would happen if the same man had a prime territory to work in. Full of optimism, he gave the fellow a much better territory but saw his overall sales effectiveness drop almost instantly. When the next year was finished, he had earned only $5,000, despite having access to much greater opportunity in the new territory.

So it continued, year after year. No matter how promising, or dismal, the salesperson's territory was, he *always* found a way to make it produce roughly $5,000 for him in commissions. One year, he was significantly ahead of quota with plenty of time still to sell, and his sales manager thought that the pattern was finally broken. No such luck. The salesperson developed a mysterious illness, spent several months out of the field, and returned to action just in time to finish the year at (you guessed it) $5,000 in commissions.

Regardless of whether he knew it, that salesperson had expectations. He saw himself as a $5,000-a-year man. What he didn't do was *manage* his expectations effectively. If he'd wanted to, he could have seen himself as a $30,000-a-year man, quite a sum for the mid-1950s, or an even higher figure. *His past did not have to determine his future.* But he allowed it to by default, because he refused to change his own expectations on a fundamental level.

Another way of looking at this, of course, is that the salesperson never had a manager who helped him to set a new, more realistic expectation of himself.

Sometimes, we sabotage ourselves by settling for "what we've always done." That salesperson's return to the homing signal of $5,000 in annual income was not a unique case, and the phenomenon of not managing one's expectations effectively is certainly not limited to the world of sales. It is, however, fairly easy to *measure* in the world of sales, and the same story has played out countless times on countless sales teams.

I suspect that most sales managers today could provide multiple examples of people on their teams who had very similar experiences. *This reflects lost opportunity for both the organization and the salesperson.* These situations only change for the better when the individuals involved work with someone who can help them to accept explicit accountability for *establishing*, not simply repeating, their own expectations. Changing an existing pattern often takes good coaching. And for most salespeople, simply raising the quota to some arbitrary number *is not good coaching.*

In the end, a coach can only help us to pose good questions. We are accountable for consciously establishing our own expectations to match the current situation, our current capacities, and our own strategic intent.

Who's Setting the Best Expectations?

The people who accept accountability for, say, 10 things that are part of their job description and
(*Continued*)

(Continued)
then accept personal accountability for five more
things all on their own are the ones who are more
likely to get the bigger bonuses and bigger raises in
this company. They're the ones who may end up
running a business of their own someday.

—Elim Chew

We have to be extremely careful with expectations,
because if we're not careful, we can train ourselves to
build our expectations around what *was* possible for us.
That is very different from what *is* possible!

Talk to People before You Set the Expectation

Setting expectations in any quantitative area, any
area you can measure, means talking to people.
Instead of simply setting down a target that makes
sense to you, you have to get buy-in. You have to ask
your team, "What can happen? What is possible?
What is within reach? How much of that can we
expect to achieve?" That's the discussion you want
to have. That's what you build your constituency on—
not the other way around: "What did we do last year?
X? Okay, let's do X plus 10 percent." You want to
define the universe of what is possible, then work
backwards.

—Nido Qubein

A LESSON IN MUTUAL EXPECTATIONS

By 1993, my window and door company had lost several million dollars. We were in deep trouble. We were hemorrhaging money, and it wasn't pretty.

One huge problem we faced was our turnaround time. Our customers really didn't like the six or eight weeks it took to get our products. I knew that one of our competitors had a guaranteed two-week turnaround and that this competitor was turning around most of its orders in a single week. This competitor was hammering our company!

We began to look for ways to measurably reduce the amount of time it took us to process, assemble, and ship out an order. Because our competition was having such success with the two-week guarantee, some of the senior executives wanted to simply issue an ultimatum to the people on the shop floor: *Change the turnaround time from six weeks to two weeks maximum . . . or else!*

If we'd said that, however, we in management would have been making a big mistake. We would have been simply holding people accountable for an expectation that we had in *our* heads: two weeks, maximum!

That would have been like telling the $5,000 salesperson that his quota was now $20,000! A grand gesture, but how effective would it have been?

Sometimes, when people think of accountability, this is all they can think of—the traumatic experience of being held accountable to someone else's goal. In this case, we took a different approach, and as a result, we got a better outcome. We chose to focus on developing *shared expectations* that were based on the situation we currently faced, our own true capacities, and our strategic intent, which was to create a better offering than our competitor.

I sat down with a diverse cross-section of the company—the senior management, the salespeople, the production supervisors, and the director of operations—and we had a team meeting. We looked closely at what was actually taking place when an order came in the door and what was actually happening on the production floor.

Remember, I had done a little research to benchmark what other companies were doing, and I knew that competitor of ours was turning around many of its orders in *one* week, not two. I kept that part of the story to myself for now. The critical point was that I knew it was *possible* to get the windows shipped in a single week. I now had to get the key people in my company to buy into that expectation on their own.

Instead of simply issuing orders to the production team or holding them accountable for a goal that they had no role in shaping, I asked them some questions: "What are all the steps in the process of making a window, and how long does each of those steps take?" The director of operations broke everything down for us, from order entry to assembly to packaging and shipping. And what he came up with when you added it all up was *four and a half days*. What did that mean? Two things. First, it meant that our production system was so inefficient that it was taking four and a half days' worth of work and stretching it out over a much longer period of time. And second, those inefficiencies had created a huge backlog of orders that was keeping people from getting to new orders in a timely manager.

During a break in the meeting, one of the senior managers said to me privately, "Well, if they've got a four-and-a-half-day job, a two-week turnaround is eminently doable. Let's make that the goal."

Again, this would have been like simply assigning a new quota to the $5,000 salesperson. I wanted the *production department* to establish its own expectations and buy into those expectations based on the new information they had.

When we returned to the meeting, I asked the director of operations, "If we had a two-week timeline to hit, that would mean an order would just be sitting here for a whole week before anything started, right?"

He thought for a moment and said, "Yes, that's right. It doesn't have to be that way. We really should be able to turn an order around in a week."

I said, "Great. What would have to happen for you to turn the orders around in that time period?"

He said, "Let me talk to our people."

We agreed that he would have an assessment for us to look at the next day.

I knew that just setting the target was not enough. I had to give him the opportunity to go to his people and give them ownership of what was going to happen on the production floor. They had to feel empowered and challenged by the new goal we were talking about, and they had to decide for themselves that the goal was realistic.

The next day, he came back with a plan for completely redesigning our order entry and production process. *It was his team's plan—not mine.* But it was based not on our current standard of performance but on the new assumption that it was possible to process, complete, and ship an order within a single business week. I okayed the plan and gave him the resources he needed to put it into action. I also gave him the authority to do what he and his team felt was necessary to turn our expectation into a reality. I asked him to let me know if a time came when it looked like the plan was going to hit a roadblock, and he accepted accountability for implementing the new plan.

Over the next six weeks, he and his team took the entire system apart and put it back together again. They streamlined everything, from the way an order came in to the way it was assembled to the way it was shipped out.

Less than a month and a half after our initial meeting, we had set up a system that placed orders into our production people's hands almost immediately. Production changed the design and flow of raw materials through the manufacturing process. We cleaned up our backlog of orders without compromising our quality in any way. All the windows were made correctly, and they were shipped within the new time standard that *our employees* had set down for themselves. We went from hemorrhaging money every month to *making* money every month.

Without shared expectations, the order-entry and production process had rambled aimlessly. With shared expectations, a quality product was being manufactured in a much shorter period of time, and our customers were happier. We probably couldn't say the same about our competition, of course, but that was their problem!

What allowed us to turn things around? I believe it was our ability to set and act on *mutual* expectations and our willingness to give the team both the responsibility and the authority they needed to do the job.

Make a Prediction

How we set our expectations for ourselves and [where] we set those expectations, or the level at
(Continued)

---

which we set them, is often determined by the people we surround ourselves with or the social context within which we make predictions about what we are likely to do. As a researcher, I've found that when I ask people to make predictions about behaviors like voting, or choosing healthy foods, or being on time, or getting their health checked, or taking their medications, I find that the act of asking them to predict what's going to happen in their own lives is actually more effective in reinforcing those kinds of behaviors than simply reminding people about the behavior. If you really want to inspire someone to take action on something worthwhile, you may want [to] consider asking the person to make a prediction to you or another person about what he or she plans to do in that area.

—Eric Spangenberg

BEYOND "WE'VE ALWAYS DONE IT THAT WAY"

What are you using to establish your expectations—your goals for yourself and your organization? If it's past precedent, or what you've always been able to do before, your expectations may not reflect your true potential, either as an individual or as an organization.

If I hadn't known that there was someone in our industry turning orders around in one week, I would not have pointed the team in that direction.

According to many of the people I interviewed, the expectations we set for ourselves should, as a general

Evaluate Your Expectations of Others

If people keep missing their expectations, they get discouraged and despondent, and it gets worse as they go along. So, you try to budget your expectations. If my magazine's salespeople keep missing the goals that I set for them, then obviously, I am doing a bad job. They will get discouraged, and sometimes they will go and do something else, which is not what I'm after. So, it is a delicate balance.

—Peter Legge

rule, be *higher* than past precedent"—"the way we have always done it."

In fact, a big part of the leader's job is to model the accountability of consistently putting precedent in context and looking toward what makes the most sense for all his or her stakeholders, now and in the future, based on what is possible today. To find out what's possible today, we must be willing to look outside our comfort zone, our business, and our industry.

Benchmark Based on What's Happening outside Your World

At our hospital, we constantly try to isolate whatever *isn't* adding value to the customer and then minimize or eliminate the problem. Our expectation is that we will continually improve on the quality of the
(*Continued*)

customer experience. When you spend four hours in a hospital, the only thing you really want to pay for is that 10 minutes you spend with the doctor when he tells you, "Here's your medication, and here's your treatment plan." Then, you want to go home. So, everything that makes you wait would ideally need to be considered "non-value-added" and eliminated. That's what we're always moving toward. We always want to identify a baseline and a metric for what the customer actually wants to experience and then look at whether we were successful in moving that needle in the right direction.

In doing that, it's been our experience that when we're deciding what should be improved and by how much, we often want to benchmark based on what's happening *outside* the hospital. We want to identify where the relevant best practice really is, and we want to know what our own expectation should be in executing that best practice. There were a lot of times where we decided to look at the auto industry, so we could benefit from something they had learned from making cars. If we had managed our expectations based only on the experiences we ourselves had lived through inside of a hospital, we would have missed out on a lot. You have to be willing to say, "You know what? There are people out there doing things we haven't even thought about. Let's go see what their journey has been, and let's see how they're doing two, or three, or five years along the maturation cycle of an idea that might apply to us." That willingness to go off campus, to set targets based on what people outside

(Continued)

> *(Continued)*
> of health care were doing, helped us to set and meet expectations that would never, ever have arisen from our own environment. And once you find evidence that it can be done, your whole expectation changes. If you only look at your own experience, you *will* self-limit.
>
> —Joan Magruder

Another standard for establishing expectations that the people I interviewed agreed on was this one: Don't set your expectations based on the *outcome* you want. Set your expectations based on the right things that will *deliver* that outcome when an individual team member performs them on a consistent basis.

What Comes *before* the Deal?

If you're thinking about selling for us, you might think that the goal you'd be working toward was to close X dollars in business. Actually, that's wrong. That's not the goal. We don't even care about that. What we care about are the five separate metrics that we are going to be measuring that *precede* you closing the deal.

If you execute against those metrics day in day out, consistently with rigor, that is all we care about and all we measure. Our expectation is for you to do those things. If you execute against those metrics, you will get to where you need to get to in terms of closed
(Continued)

> sales. And if for some reason you don't get to where you want [to] get to on the income side, then it is not your fault. It is our fault. We either screwed up your target list, or we didn't train you appropriately, or our strategy was wrong. The expectation is never the end goal, because by then, it is too late.
>
> —Brian Martin

Do some benchmarking. Know what the expectation should be, and don't be afraid to point beyond your own past experience in setting a new expectation. Get the team involved, pose good questions, and the team will often set the expectations even higher than you would.

> ## Stretch Your Expectations
>
> Every day, you have the opportunity to do things that you never thought you could accomplish—but that means getting out of your comfort zone and experiencing all the discomfort in learning, growing, failing, and striving in order to reach new levels. It may also mean trying to ratchet up the expectations someone has set for you instead of dumbing them down.
>
> —Jim McCool

If you are in senior management, remember that pushing beyond what's realistic can set your team up for failure. The team has to know that your expectations, while aggressive, are grounded in reality. They must also know that you are committed to the expectation, that you are enthusiastic about it, and that you are allocating appropriate resources to support them as they turn the expectation into reality.

Get Full Value from Your Expectations

If you set expectations too high, you are not going to get the full value out of your people. If you set expectations too *low*, you're not getting the full value, either. You have to create a certain amount of tension in terms of your expectations, but not too much. I think that a big challenge that a lot of business leaders have is that we set our expectations for others based on what we expect of ourselves. It is unreasonable for leaders to expect exactly the same things of others that they expect of themselves. Even in my own business, I used to get frustrated that people were not living up to the standards that I had set. I eventually realized that the standards were the same ones I had set for myself. Well, I don't really have any right to expect them to do what I do in terms of the work hours or the effort. I have everything to win and everything to lose; it's my business. When I chose to build and grow a business and chose to work nights and weekends when I needed to, I put myself in a separate category. If I'm going to set expectations that other people are going to buy into, I need to accept that other people haven't made that choice.

—David Silverstein

Beware of team expectations that have been set by a single individual. Get feedback from all the stakeholders, and get a look at relevant benchmarks from other industries, companies, and functional areas.

DO YOUR EXPECTATIONS SUPPORT YOUR VALUES?

Of course, raising the right expectations applies not just to performance benchmarks but also to your team's values and ethical standards. If you put all your time, effort, attention, and energy into the production side, but you don't tie those performance targets into your organization's values and ethical expectations, you will inevitably face problems. The values must always guide the performance targets! If they don't, you've got an *expectations mismatch*.

Use Expectations to Support Your Values

I believe that no business is successful without good procedures. Initially, those procedures are likely to incorporate good values. What happens, though, over time, is that as an organization grows, people forget to expand their procedures in a way that supports the organization's values, and as a result, some companies put their employees in a bad situation: They don't give them the backing or the information or the resources they need to make those values a reality.

(Continued)

(Continued)
You need something that says to the employee, "Look, even if the client wants to do this, you tell them no." We would rather lose the business than do something that would put our values in question.

—Greg Powell

No organization is sustainable without values to complement and guide the performance expectations it gives its team members. If your organization avoids dealing with an expectations mismatch for long enough, it will inevitably end up facing a crisis.

Let Your People Tell You When the Values Are in Conflict with the Expectation

We sometimes forget that there is a potential major problem with expectations that are too high—that are not in alignment with what can actually be achieved. This is where integrity starts to play a role. It may be possible that others may set your expectations higher than are realistic. At that point, you have to be willing to demonstrate enough integrity to push back a little and say, "You know what? I can't achieve at that level, and we need to talk about that now."

If you look at the most spectacular frauds that have been committed in various business settings over the

(Continued)

---

last 20 years, you find that there are a number of cases you can trace back to the fact that people were being "held accountable" for achieving things they could only achieve by bending or breaking the rules. The expectations were never benchmarked. If the pressure gets very intense, for instance, to deliver a certain level of earnings per share, people may conclude that they have to start to bend the rules and to cheat in order to do that. That's not what we want. We want them to have a place where they can step up and say to someone in authority that it's simply not possible to hit the goal without compromising standards that shouldn't be compromised. They shouldn't be punished for saying that out loud.

What you have to watch out for is when you develop a culture of management consistently saying, "Look, we don't care if there are no benchmarks that support the idea of attaining this goal; if you're going to work here, you're going to find a way to go out and do it, and how you pull that off is your problem. Don't bother me with the details." If the expectations become suddenly unachievable, or more importantly, if they were never achievable in the first place, then you have to be willing to let people have an honest conversation with you about that.

—Richard Chambers

ACCOUNTABILITY CHECK!

Now, it's time to expand your Accountability Zone.

Implement what you have learned about the fourth accountability.

Your primary accountability check: Look for benchmarks *outside your industry, functional circle, or area of expertise* that will tell you where your most critical expectations should be set. For instance, if you are a manager in charge of a hotel, what could you learn from the cruise ship industry about expectations in the areas of customer service, restaurant management, hospitality, room service delivery time, and guest satisfaction? If you own and operate a home-based writing business, what expectations could you set for yourself in the areas of accounting, promotion/marketing, or time management by talking to someone who operates a home-based graphic design business?

Individual focus: Identify your own personal expectations for the next 30 days. Don't set arbitrary goals—set targets that you know from your own personal experience and research that you can hit, want to hit, and will know when you have hit.

- *How* do you know this expectation is attainable? (What outside source confirms this? Who could you talk to for benchmarking purposes? Identify at least three candidates.)

- *Why* do you want to fulfill this expectation? (What is the reason to take action on it today and for the next 30 days?)
- *What* will tell you for certain that you have actually attained this goal? (Will your bank account be at a certain level? Will your production increase in a measurable way? Will your weight be at a certain number of pounds and no higher?

Team or organization focus: Pick one *measurable* expectation that your team is supposed to execute on. Then do the following.

- Identify at least three outside organizations you could evaluate for benchmarking purposes in setting this expectation. Don't be afraid to choose organizations that are outside your industry circle.
- Make a list of all the stakeholders, both internal and external, who will be affected by your team's hitting (or failing to hit) this goal. This includes each of your team members!
- Place a check mark by every stakeholder who has given you feedback (such as an e-mail or a brief verbal assessment) on whether the expectation you have established is appropriate. Ask for advice on establishing the expectation. Look for benchmarks.
- Make sure you receive some form of feedback from *every* stakeholder you can track down before you confirm the expectation. Is the goal too high or too low? Does what you're trying to accomplish support the organization's strategic intent? Do you have buy-in? Does your expectation support your organization's values?

7

THE FIFTH ACCOUNTABILITY: CONTRIBUTING TO YOUR RELATIONSHIPS

T he final accountability involves our relationships with others and with the larger world. Failure to manage our relationships means ultimate failure. Success in managing our relationships means ultimate success. This success or failure depends entirely on the quality of our contributions.

Relationships at Many Levels

We are all accountable to stakeholders. As dean, I have different groups of stakeholders, each in a different stage of their relationship with my organization, which is a business school. I have to pull all of those folks

(Continued)

(Continued)
together and integrate them in a way that creates a
critical mass support for our programs, whether it be
financial support, or support in terms of activity and
involvement, or other kinds of support. My job is
really about maintaining relationships, developing
new relationships, and most importantly, engaging
those relationships in a way that creates the energy
and the outcomes that we are looking for. So, for
example, I need to maintain relationships with perspective students. These are students that haven't
yet decided to come to my university, but at the
same time, they are looking at it. I need to be able
to engage them and maintain relationships with
them so that they will eventually decide to come
here. That means giving something to that relationship, of course. I need to maintain that relationship
and build it into a different type of relationship.
Ideally, they turn into students, and I engage with
them on that front as well. When those students
leave this place, they become alumni of the university. That's a completely different set of stakeholders
and a different part of the evolution as these people
go through the system.

As alumni get further away from the school in
terms of years, they often become financially successful, and they have the capacity to become donors, and perhaps even major donors. So, I have to
manage those relationships as well. And then often,
past the donor stage, many of these folks begin to
think about where they are going to send their
(Continued)

children to school, and so the cycle starts all over
again. And so for me, my job, and any success I have
experienced in my job, [it] is all about maintaining
accountability to those relationships and integrating
those relationships with the school.

—Beck Taylor

We are each accountable to make contributions to our
relationships. In fact, making a contribution is the *only*
effective way to manage a relationship.

As individuals, we are accountable to *ourselves* for each
of the other four accountabilities. At the same time, we are
accountable to others in our lives. We all have important
connections and commitments to other people, either
individually or collectively.

Stop and think about any great accomplishment or
positive event in your life. Whether it was your graduation, a promotion, starting your own company, or any
other landmark, you didn't experience it entirely on your
own. Whatever that achievement or positive experience
was, it involved someone else. Once you understand
this much about human experience, you begin to understand why the ultimate punishment in any penal system,
short of the death penalty itself, is solitary confinement.
When society really wants to make a point, it doesn't
add years to a wrongdoer's sentence or work hours to
the man or woman's day: It deprives the wrongdoer of
relationships.

Our accountabilities to manage our relationships come
in two big categories. First, we need to contribute to our
personal relationships with family, friends, and business

You Are Accountable for the Quality
of the Relationship

Malcolm Gladwell writes about the fact that a given doctor's likelihood of being sued by a patient has very little to do with the competency of the doctor and almost everything to do with the quality of the relationship the doctor has with the patient. We may lose sight of the importance of the doctor being accountable for supporting the relationship. If I was going to practice with 20 physicians, I would want to make sure that my peers were going to be held accountable for doing a good job when it comes to managing their relationships, in addition to being held accountable for the practice of good medicine.

In the workplace, I expect my employees to do a good job of managing their relationships with others. It's part of their job. It matters. I have let many a person go who was doing a good job as an individual contributor but thought it was unimportant to manage relationships with other people. They would say, "Leave me alone! I do my job well; nothing else should matter. I don't care what other people think." It absolutely does matter what other people think. You shouldn't compromise your ethics or compromise who you are, but you have to realize that it really does matter what other people think of you.

—David Silverstein

associates. This falls under the heading of *personal accountability*. We also need to contribute to our relationships with society and the larger world in which we live. This falls under the category of *social accountability*.

In both realms, we should constantly be looking for ways to *invest* in the relationship and enhance the value of the relationship over time.

The secret of successful relationship management in terms of both personal accountability and social accountability can be summed up in one word: *give*.

Try this simple experiment: Think of a single important, successful relationship in your own life that *does not* feature you making some kind of contribution or the other person making some kind of contribution to you. It should take you about 30 seconds to realize that the only relationships that fall into this category are *dead* ones. In fact, the quickest way to *kill* a relationship is to start keeping track of all the reasons it's not your turn to give to it and support it. *The minute two people stop looking for reasons to give to each other, the relationship between those two people starts to decline.*

Personal accountability is not about giving back—it's about giving!

If you're truly accountable to a personal relationship, you will give—period. You will look for reasons to serve others.

How do you treat the key relationships in your life? Do you look for reasons to give, period? Or, do you look for reasons to give *because you feel you owe someone something*? There's a big difference, you know. The kind of giving that supports relationships is the giving that doesn't think about what's gone before or what's likely to come back in return.

Giving back is the process of giving because you have received something first. That kind of giving is not based on the core principle of giving because it is the right thing to do. Whether you have received something first should not enter into your decision to give. The cycle of real giving in any relationship always begins with the *intent* to give.

Real giving has to start with someone asking, "What can I give to this relationship?" Why shouldn't that someone be you?

This kind of giving always pays off in the long term. When I was in the window business, there were times when there were industry-wide glass shortages, but the relationships we had contributed to over time saw us through. We had built up strong personal relationships with our key vendors, and because we had held ourselves accountable for maintaining those relationships over time, everything was in place when we needed glass. When there were shortages, we never ran out of glass. We sometimes ran low, but we never ran out.

Supporting Relationships over Time

Getting is often a result of giving, but if the giving is an expectation to get something, then it comes across as a hollow kind of giving. Most of our company's suppliers turn into lifelong friends, because we really want to help them and help their businesses. As a result, most of our supplier relationships have gotten better and better over time.

(Continued)

> During the recession recently, things fell off the cliff for everybody, and businesses slowed down for a lot of our suppliers. There were companies that flooded the market with inventories; people were going bankrupt. We could have bought that inventory and changed suppliers over and over again, but we decided that we are going to stick with the long term, stay with the people who had helped us to put together a winning formula, and support our long-term suppliers. We built a plan together with our key supplier to win in our market. That plan didn't make them liquidate their entire inventory, because we knew that wasn't a good approach in the long term. We decided that we weren't going to play that game, and we decided we were going to commit to the relationship.
>
> —Jeff Booth

There is something fundamentally human about acknowledging the fifth accountability. We are built with the need to connect with others, the need to nurture and sustain relationships, and the need to care and be cared about. We are somehow more ourselves when we make a conscious choice to give something to a relationship with someone else. The relationships that matter most to us are the ones in which *both* sides are accountable, over time, for giving to the relationship *for the sake of the relationship itself.*

Any meaningful relationship that endures over time inevitably draws on this sense of mutual accountability. The more individual accountability there is for giving within any relationship—not giving back, but giving—the more significant the relationship is to both parties.

Supporting Relationships over Time

Managing relationships will always be an essential part of leadership. Leaders can't act effectively without good advice from reliable sources, and you can't get that advice without giving something to the relationship. Whenever you act as a leader, you have to make sure you keep your people on board—people who may agree or disagree with the course you're pursuing at any given moment. It's a little like a marriage. You can't simply ignore your spouse.

In our case, we were negotiating a new constitution on behalf of 42 million people. Managing relationships in that situation is not always easy. In fact, it's often easier to negotiate with your opponents than with those who are supposed to be your supporters. You have to work hard on an ongoing basis to stay connected, because you need people who are close to you and who will tell you what you need to hear, even though it may not be what you want to hear. You want close counterparts—people who are willing to be transparent in their thinking; people who are prepared to share what they think and accountable for what they have said to you in the past.

—Roelf Meyer

YOUR SPHERE OF CONTRIBUTION MODELS YOUR VALUES

In your personal life, what are you doing to support the people you love and care about?

If you're a salesperson, what are you doing proactively to connect and reconnect with your clients?

If you're in management, what are you doing to find out what's going on in the lives of the people on your team? What are you doing to help them achieve their goals?

Building relationships is about choices, and the choices should always be based on your values. To get a fix on your values, ask yourself: How can I best serve this relationship in the short term *and* the long term? Posing that question on a consistent basis allows you to create a group of values-based connections, which I call your *sphere of contribution*.

When you're expanding your sphere of contribution, you're not focused on short-term agendas. Serving effectively in both the short and long terms becomes your overarching purpose—your standard for managing all of your relationships. Once you're committed to serving effectively, your decisions suddenly get a whole lot easier, because your best values are driving the actions that serve the people you're connected to.

When I'm training senior executives in the *No More Excuses* program to create a culture of accountability in their organization, they often ask me about the best ways to cultivate ethical, responsible, transparent decision making. The answer isn't to write a memo or give a lecture. It's to give, give, and give some more to the people who are closest to you in the organization.

Any organization's commitment to social responsibility can only be a reflection of the responsibility its people demonstrate to their colleagues *within* the organization.

When there are challenges in your relationships, find new solutions that work in the long term, in the light of day, and with everyone looking. When there are problems,

---

Delivering on the Promise

Our promise at High Point is, "Every student receives an extraordinary education in a fun environment with caring people." That means we're accountable to each other for delivering on being caring. So, how do you do that? Well, you do it in small ways and big ways, and you start by recognizing that the caring doesn't stop with our relationships with the students. If we don't exhibit that caring internally, we can't possibly show it to our students. So, for instance, we just built a building that was supposed to cost $40 million; it ended up costing over $60 million. I'm now accountable to explaining to the Finance Committee Board of Trustees and to other stakeholders exactly how and why that happened, how I plan to deal with it, and why the end result is going to be fruitful, purposeful, and worthy of any risk that was invested in the process.

If I'm going to be true to our promise and our mission, I have to accept both the accountability for that project and also the accountability to be caring toward the other people in the organization with whom I'm working.

—Nido Qubein

---

acknowledge them openly, accept your fair share of the responsibility for resolving them, and spend more time on the *solution* than on the blame game.

If you take that approach, your team will follow your own example. They'll start asking how they can best serve the relationship and the organization in both the short *and* long terms, and they will never, ever solve a problem in a way they wouldn't want to read about tomorrow morning on the front page of *USA Today*.

Lecturing people about values is useless. Using the contributions you make to a relationship to *model* your values is a much more effective strategy. In the end, for any organization to endure, our accountability to manage our relationships must support principles of equity, transparency, and ethical dealings with others.

No Transparency, No Accountability

You cannot have an ethical behavior unless you actually are accountable or transparent about what you do. You cannot say, "I behave ethically, but I don't bother to disclose what I do."

—Jordi Canals

NETWORK BY GIVING

Don't worry about widening your sphere of influence. Focus on widening your *sphere of contribution*. That's the sum total of the people you have a connection with and are willing to give something to on a consistent basis. Your sphere of contribution should be aligned with your values and should be constantly expanding. You should always be looking for new people you can give to and connect with. The more people you help succeed today, the more people who will be out there predisposed to help you succeed tomorrow.

The only truly effective way to network is to *give* to a relationship within your sphere of contribution and then *connect* that relationship to another great relationship in a way that benefits everyone involved. In essence, you're giving again by introducing people. On social networking sites like YouTube and LinkedIn, you can do this in a matter of seconds with a few clicks of your mouse.

As I was writing this book, I used Twitter to send a message to my contact base about an interview I wanted to conduct. Within seconds, I received a response from one of the people on my list, and in just a few minutes, I had a new interview and a brand new professional contact!

JUST KEEP GIVING

Just keep giving to the people in your sphere. Give time, give energy, give thought, and give care. Just keep giving, and the relationships will grow. Don't worry about what's coming back to you. Get better at giving than anyone else. This is one of the classic secrets of leadership. It's something that every leader I interviewed was eager to share. I don't know how much of a secret this really is, but it's definitely a principle observed by highly accountable executives and managers at all levels.

Have you noticed that the most effective businesses tend to be led by great networkers? These are people who stand out *because* they know how to *give* to relationships. Those leaders never take any relationships for granted. They know that all human relationships, whether high or low, are based on contributions, and they are always looking for some reason to give. That's networking!

Suppose you're a salesperson taking an important client out to lunch. Granted, you're having lunch because this individual is a client. If you're truly connected to that person as a person, however, and if you're truly looking for ways to support and make contributions to the relationship, more often than not, you will find that the business will take care of itself! This is the secret of most successful sales careers: The salesperson cares about the customer as a person and is personally accountable for looking for ways to make contributions to the relationship.

As you grow your relationships, you inevitably grow your sphere of contribution. For this book, I interviewed a lot of people—many of whom reached out to other people who were intrigued by the possibility of taking part in the project. I was introduced to people from all over the world and from all walks of life who were as enthusiastic as I was about the subject of accountability. By the time I was done writing the book, I had many more relationships than I had when I started out and many more opportunities to give.

Don't get distracted by networking. Just keep looking for new ways to give and new contributions you can make to the relationships that you have in your life. *Your sphere of contribution will grow and thrive, and so will you.* The more focused you are on giving *for the sake of giving*, the better off everyone in your sphere of contribution will be.

Giving to Stakeholders

Every three months, I communicated with our entire employee pool by sending out a personal letter. I
(Continued)

(Continued)

wrote not to the employee but to the employee's family to tell everyone how the company was doing. If profit sharing was on track, we included a little check for every family. I think it was $175 every three months. That's not a big deal from an accounting standpoint, but from a relationship standpoint, it was everything. To get a letter from the president of the company, along with a check—it was very meaningful to the relationship.

Another relationship strategy I used: When I was taking a flight, I'd have them make an announcement at the terminal: "The CEO of our airline is at Gate 12; he will be here for about 10 or 15 minutes. If any of you have a question about Southwest Airlines, please stop by and say hello to our president." Many times, 10 or 15 people would show up, and I would shake a few hands. Just making that interaction proactively built up the relationships and improved our connections with people.

—Howard Putnam

Supporting relationships with stakeholders is an art, not a science. It requires engagement on many fronts, and it means being willing to connect with employees, customers, and others on a personal level. If you do not respect a relationship enough to send the message that you actually care about a stakeholder's emotions, you are not yet fully accountable for supporting that relationship.

"Our Emotions Are Our Reality"

We are all human beings, and that means we experience nothing aside from our emotions. Our emotions are our reality. So, if you're going to manage relationships, you've got to manage emotions. I have asked every single person I've hired two questions: "First, what is most important for you to feel professionally, every day? And second, what's most important for you to *avoid* feeling? What would you really rather not go through, not have to replay with your spouse at the end of the day, when that person asks how your day went?" I keep the answers on file, and I look at those answers every week when I do my own planning.

I always try to remind myself that I'm not so much "managing people" as I am managing what they want on an emotional level. When you realize what it is that they want, you also realize that you have to talk to each person in a unique way.

—Brian Martin

WHO BUILT THE WELL?

I got up this morning, and the first thing I did was to go into the bathroom, turn on the faucet, fill a glass with water, and brush my teeth. As I was doing that, I started thinking: *Water is the sustaining force of all life. We simply cannot live without water. Who built the system that gets the water onto my toothbrush?* I didn't have the slightest idea.

Then, I began thinking that not so very long ago, people weren't fortunate enough to be able to simply turn on the faucet every time they needed water. What did they do? They went out to the well and they *pumped* some water. And if you lived in a small community, maybe at the center of the community was a town well. Everyone in the community drew water from that well, and everyone benefited from the well. But you know what? The people using the well often aren't the same people who dug the well.

Think about that for a minute. Think about what was happening just a century ago in this country. The people in a town were drinking water and sustaining life from something that had been created before they even existed. Had someone not dug that well, the town would not be able to support itself! We take things like that for granted sometimes.

Someone always has to start digging the well. If you stop and take a look around, you'll realize there are a lot of wells waiting to be dug these days.

Barack Obama once said, "We are the people we've been waiting for." That's another way of saying that *someone* always has to start the giving, and I see him every morning in the mirror when I turn on my water faucet and start brushing my teeth!

We are each responsible, not just for ourselves but for the larger good.

Finding Purpose

What gives human life purpose? I think it's our passionate pursuit of something that can define our legacy
(Continued)

---

in a meaningful, purposeful way that involves service. You just have to choose what you want to do to serve. Whatever you choose, pursue it in a way that stretches you a little. Every time you stretch beyond yourself, you redefine who you really are. Whether you're successful in your aim is almost secondary. What matters is the continuous, tenacious commitment to make something happen that will allow you to serve someone or something that's bigger than you are.

I have tried to spend a third of my life earning, a third of my life learning, and a third of my life serving— and looking back, I realize I've gotten the most profound happiness and satisfaction from the serving part of that equation. Not everyone who is materially successful is happy. Once you look at those who are both materially successful *and* happy, what you will find is that their happiness is almost always rooted in their ability to serve—their ability to build bridges and connect with other people and benefit those people.

I believe that at the end of the day, we really are accountable for our gifts—for the abundance that has been given to us. I believe we benefit most when we benefit others.

—Nido Qubein

For many, the fifth accountability's emphasis on selfless giving takes on a spiritual dimension. That was certainly the case with many of the people I interviewed for this book.

"The Ultimate Accountability"

Be your best, not just for yourself but for others as well. Ask yourself: What is my purpose? If the answer is "making a lot of money," then you may have a situation where greed undercuts accountability. If I am too greedy, then I won't be responsible to my community, my country, or my world. I think the happiest people are those who are not just searching for money but want to contribute something to others. The ultimate accountability, I think, is to observe the Golden Rule.
—Tan Sri Ramon V. Navaratnam

In the end, regardless of whether we give ourselves a spiritual reason for doing so, we have to give something; not necessarily money, but *something*. We can give time, we can give attention, or we can give the recycled aluminum cans we find by the side of the road. Again, this is not *giving back* to the community but simply *giving*: giving for its own sake, for the greater good. It's like digging a well for people who will be drinking from it in the future who we may never meet.

A Billion Trees

Ultimately, I feel that we are accountable to our internal and external customers, to our community, and ultimately, to our planet. We must be accountable for giving something to the planet we live in. That's
(Continued)

---

probably the highest level of accountability for me. My goal is to plant a billion trees; we're pursuing that goal on our web site, www.saveourplanet.org. I think that's part of being accountable to the environment—taking on the responsibility to bring oxygen back to the environment.

In the end, it's all about giving: not just giving money but giving time and being involved—actually being part of the community. Sometimes when people get too greedy, it's because they've forgotten about someone that they were supposed to be accountable to. That's where a lot of the problems in the financial sector and in other parts of the global economy sprang from, I think. People forgot about their own accountability to their internal and external customers, and to the larger community, and to the planet.

—Dato' Dr. Jannie Tay

For many of the Accountability Masters I talked to, the fifth accountability took the form of a desire to contribute, not just to those who were close to them personally but to all those who cannot help themselves.

"Am I My Brother's Keeper?"

I was interviewed about my contribution to the disadvantaged people in Puerto Rico. The person asked me to sum up my beliefs, and I quoted a story from the Bible. In the Bible, when Cain killed Abel and God
(Continued)

(*Continued*)
asked him about his brother, Cain asked back, "Am I my brother's keeper?" Yes, we are, and isn't it wonderful that we are? We are blessed that we are. What an honor and a joy.

—Sila Calderón

SOCIAL ACCOUNTABILITY

We each have a relationship with our community, and the best way to nurture that relationship is to give. You don't have to give money, but you do have to give something.

Making a Difference

I always ask the question, "Is what I am doing making a difference?" I try to remember what was helpful to me, and then I try to do that for others.

—Lowell Kruse

Community can be the local Parent Teacher Association, the township you live in, your subdivision, your church or synagogue, or a food pantry in your community. These days, with the Internet, our community is not only going to be local but also global, and for all I know, intergalactic.

Community may include people I do not know. It may be the future community that comes along after I'm gone. I'm accountable for devoting time to digging wells and creating opportunities for the people who are coming along in a generation or two, and so are you. We are accountable to the people who need a hand getting started or the people who are just plain down and out and don't know where to turn. Each of us has *something* to give. Each of us has *some* time. Each of us could watch one less television show a week and find a way to help out somehow, somewhere.

Green Accountability

Sometimes, giving means taking less. We found out that we were the biggest user of power in the city of Sydney, Australia, and we realized that that put us in a position where we really wanted to look more closely at what we were doing. What we found is that our greatest opportunities for cutting down our own energy use lay in the heating ventilation and air conditioning area, where we can reduce our power consumptions by 20 percent. We set that goal for ourselves, and now we are making good progress.

—Steve Roper

There is always a great opportunity to follow through on the fifth accountability, support a relationship, and find something to give. The question is whether we are willing to look for that opportunity.

There are many different ways to contribute. If we actually think we do not have an opportunity to give, then we have left the Accountability Zone.

Change Your Perspective

A friend told me once, "When I get rich, I want to be one of those people who gives and gives at every opportunity." I told him he had it backwards. The wealthiest people I know—and I'm not just talking about wealth in monetary terms—are wealthy *because* they are always looking for opportunities to give. That's how they got there.

—Jeff Booth

You can start by finding more opportunities to give just a little of the most precious commodity of all: your time. We are each given 24 hours in a day. We can each choose to give some portion of that time to a cause that is larger than ourselves.

No Excuses for Not Giving

People tell me they can't afford to give. They say, "Hey, I have no money. I can't do what you do." Okay— give some time. Just because you don't have the dollars to throw around right now, that's no excuse for not giving. If you can't give money, give your time, or give your attention. Time is just as good as money, and in many cases, probably a lot better.

When I was about 21 years old, I had no money to give, but I agreed to give a lot of my time to the Big

(Continued)

Brothers and Big Sisters of America. I think I made a real difference in one kid's life. His name was Andrew. I worked with him for two straight years, every Saturday, and at the end of our time together, he was enrolling in technical school. He wasn't on drugs; he wasn't stealing anything; he wasn't hanging out with the wrong crowd. He was on the right track. Looking back, I like to think the time we spent together on Saturday afternoons was a part of him being on the right track. That wasn't any kind of financial gift at all. It was just deciding to spend time with Andrew instead of watching the ball game on Saturday afternoon.

Everybody has some time to give. Nobody is that busy. If you think you don't have time to give, just keep track of the amount of time you spend watching TV or looking at YouTube. Everybody is given 24 hours in a day, 365 days a year. The question is, what do we want to do with those 24 hours? You can choose to make a difference with your time.

One really important rule when it comes to giving is follow-through. If you say you are going to do something, then show up and do it. Anyone can talk about giving; not everyone actually gives. I have a little saying: "Talk is cheap; whiskey costs money." So, don't just talk! Put something on the table after you make a commitment, whether it's money or your own involvement or a combination of the two.

Find something you can make a commitment to—and then follow through on that commitment. Show up and do something.

—Michael Staenberg

Show Them What Your Company Believes about Relationships

A customer who had bought four shirts returned to one of our stores after she noticed that she'd lost her wallet. She didn't have any money to get home. Our employee decided to loan the customer $50 from the cash register. The next day, the customer and her parents came into the store and repaid the money. That employee not only won us a customer for life by choosing to support that relationship—she modeled our company culture for everyone else in our organization.

—Elim Chew

And of course, we can give by making a long-term personal commitment to help our neighborhood, our community, our nation, and the larger world in which we live. In doing so, we are expanding our Accountability Zone in the most profound way of all—by acknowledging that we are connected to countless others and that everything that touches us ultimately touches another person.

Change the World by Making a Personal Commitment

In South Africa, we have a lot of poor people. We have someone begging on every single corner at every single traffic light in the city. You constantly feel

(Continued)

> the need to help the wider community, and I think as a world, we have to do that. It doesn't make sense to me that a third of the children in this country are living on a starvation diet—that is unacceptable. I think the greatest accountability I would have above all the others would be to make sure that we as a world do not allow that to continue for much longer.
>
> —Gary Bailey

ACCOUNTABILITY CHECK!

Now, it's time to expand your Accountability Zone.

Implement what you have learned about the fifth accountability.

Your primary accountability: Identify at least three instances when you have reached out to help someone with no expectation of receiving help in return. If you can't think of three, *make those three contributions right now!*

Individual focus: Pick one person who is extremely close to you and one person who isn't. Give each a voice-to-voice call today that lets the person know you are thinking of him or her and hoping all is well. Keep calling until you reach someone live—don't leave a voice-mail message. *Do not ask that person to do anything for you or even imply that he or she should do something for you!*

- List 10 important relationships on a sheet of paper. For each one, write down what you've done to support each of those relationships and when you've done it. Then, list what you plan to do next to make a contribution to each relationship.
- Identify at least one opportunity where you can personally make a contribution to the larger community—without having been asked.
- *We are all accountable to someone!* To whom will you be accountable (besides yourself) for taking action on your plan for supporting or contributing to your relationships?

Team or organization focus: Identify one way your team, department, or company can give something of value to the larger community. Come up with an idea for something you aren't already doing *and* have not been asked to do. Discuss your idea with your team, and come up with an action plan for giving time, effort, energy, or resources that reflects your organizational values and priorities. Review your plan with the team on a daily, weekly, or monthly basis.

8

CREATING A CULTURE OF ACCOUNTABILITY

There were so many great insights from my interviews with the Accountability Masters that I was tempted to start work on a sequel before I even finished this book.

The wealth of great material at my disposal meant that I had to think carefully about what I wanted to include in this chapter. I decided to focus on a topic that is near and dear to my heart and important to every person I interviewed: expanding the team's Accountability Zone over time by creating a long-term *culture* of accountability within the enterprise.

Everyone I interviewed for this book was a leader. Everyone I talked to was interested in making accountability a day-to-day organizational reality, not a fad or a trend or even a high priority for a single project. Everyone I talked to had already spent a great deal of time thinking about the very best ways of making accountability a way of doing business and an operating philosophy over both the short and the long term that supports the organization's mission.

Maybe you're curious as well: How *do* you implement accountability in the long run? How do you make it part of your culture? How do you keep what you've learned about the Five Accountabilities from becoming something you talk about but don't actually do? How do you ensure that accountability actually gets woven into your own life, the lives of your loved ones, and ideally, the daily life of everyone with whom you interact in the workplace during the day?

On the following pages, you will find some of my favorite responses to these questions. *Implement* what follows, and make accountability a consistent part of your own organization's culture!

MAKE ACCOUNTABILITY PART OF YOUR CULTURE BY . . . BEING CLEAR

Begin at the beginning: Building and supporting a culture of accountability starts with accepting the responsibility for clarity in your relationships with people.

Create Clarity!

If you don't have clarity, then how can you have accountability? A leader's first job, in my view, is clarity creation around business objectives and success definitions. Once you've done that, you can focus your energies on your team and the work toward attaining your objectives—not before.

—Jim McCool

MAKE ACCOUNTABILITY PART OF YOUR CULTURE BY . . . EDUCATING PEOPLE ABOUT THE "WHY" OF YOUR STRATEGIC INTENT

If your people don't understand why your organization is doing what it is doing, there is no way they are going to buy into it. If you are a leader, it is your responsibility to share the "why" behind your organization's strategic intent and to do so in a compelling way.

Do They Know Why They're Doing What They're Doing?

First of all, you must treat your employees like human beings; you must make them feel that they're actually part of the business. That means making sure they're fully aware of what the business is: why it runs the way it does, how its investments work, who the stakeholders are, and why it makes sense for them to pull together and maximize their advantage. Particularly in the African context, we have a lot of work to do on this front. Many of our mine workers see themselves simply as hands. I'll ask people, "What are you doing in this business?" And they'll say, "I'm here to sell my hands." They don't see themselves as human. They're a pair of hands that can be rented. They're physical energy that can be used in a certain way. They don't yet know why we're doing any of this. So, if you can tap into the fact that they are humans; if you can help them understand how they're using their intellect as

(Continued)

> (*Continued*)
> well as their energy and hands; if you can show them
> how they can improve the business and improve the
> outcome for themselves through improving the busi-
> ness, then suddenly you have the possibility of ac-
> countability. Now, they believe in the business. They
> didn't believe in it before—not because they were
> opposed to you, but because they didn't understand
> what you were doing. No one had explained it to them.
> So, accountability was impossible.
>
> —Gareth Taylor

MAKE ACCOUNTABILITY PART OF YOUR CULTURE BY . . . REWARDING THE RIGHT PROCESS

Earlier, we talked about managing the process, by which
we meant responding creatively to obstacles in a way that
supports your creative intent. Here, we are talking about
something very different. We are talking about rewarding
specific processes that *people find pleasurable to execute*
as they fulfill their strategic intent.

Each member of your team should enjoy moving toward
the fulfillment of his or her goals. If they don't take pleasure
in the processes that allow them to fulfill their commitments to themselves, they'll quickly lose focus. Even if their
intentions are good, they'll probably find themselves side-
lined when they hit a roadblock. It follows that if we want
a team or a person to remain accountable for taking
action on the strategic intent we've established together,
we have to make a special effort to notice, reward, and
reinforce those processes that people actually like!

No Satisfaction, No Progress

Often, people don't take enough intrinsic satisfaction out of process. Woody Allen once said that 80 percent of success is showing up. I think a lot of the time we don't stop to ask ourselves *why* people sometimes don't even bother to show up. It's because there's no satisfaction in executing the process.

If I actually have self-accountability with the short-term tactics that support my goal, I should be taking satisfaction in consistently executing that process. That has to be one of the things the process does: reengage me. I may still be nine years from my ultimate goal, but if I don't take some kind of pleasure in the process of executing, there's going to be this sense of inertia. Time will pass, and I may be sitting in the same place I was four years earlier. Too often, I think, people don't take pleasure or satisfaction in a process well executed.

—Eric Spangenberg

LEARN TOGETHER AND GROW TOGETHER

Does your organization reward learning, even when (especially when) that learning is accompanied by major mistakes? Do people in your organization know that they will be praised, not punished, for admitting that they don't know something? Do you make a point of giving people public praise for identifying major problems so that the intelligence of the enterprise as a whole can be applied to the problem?

If your answer to any of those questions was no (or even "Let me think about it"), your enterprise's culture actually makes it difficult for people to learn and grow over time. If you want people to develop full accountability, you must make it easy for them to answer for both successes and failures and to look for learning opportunities in both. (By the way, they'll learn a lot more from their failures than from their successes.)

A Lesson from Africa

Our company culture is built around a native African phrase: "Sikhula KunYe," meaning "We grow together." This is an idea we talk about almost every day: We try to empower people to make and design their own plans and then execute on those plans. We understand that this freedom also carries with it the burden of accountability. So, it may be a bit of an expensive freedom, but it's the kind of freedom we want everyone to have—not just leaders or middle management.

We want all of our people to be able to think for themselves, to be honest about both successes and failures, and to learn from what's happening. We want honest feedback, because we think that's the only way for people to learn and for the organization to learn. Blame doesn't come into play in our company except in really extraordinary situations, like corruption or gross negligence. Those are quite rare, of course. Beyond those situations, we try not to blame anybody for anything. We have this saying: "It's okay to give me the bad news immediately." That means you won't get blamed,

(Continued)

> you won't get in trouble for doing that. You know, if time is tight, just pass along the bad news, so we can do something about it. We can always talk about the good news when we see each other again. That's fine. Maybe we can have a drink together then, too.
>
> —Geotge Steyn

MAKE ACCOUNTABILITY PART OF YOUR CULTURE BY ... LETTING PEOPLE PLAY TO THEIR STRONG SUITS

The process you select for your people should be one that allows them to maximize their strong suits. If you ask them to invest their time, effort, and energy in a process they cannot execute well or cannot execute at all, they will eventually disengage. If you allow each person to use tactics that work for them, they will become more and more committed to the strategic intent you want them to buy into.

> ## Know What They Can Do ... and What They Can't
>
> I always tried to get very, very clear on what I could do and could not do in my athletic career. For instance, I knew I was shorter than most guys I played against. I had to strengthen things that would help me compensate for that. I also knew I wasn't the speediest guy in the league, and I wasn't going to become that
> *(Continued)*

(Continued)

guy anytime soon. I had longer arms and powerful legs but didn't have the quickness of some of the people I would play against. Knowing what I could do and couldn't do allowed me to focus in on those techniques that would support the things I actually *could* do to turn a game around—which in turn made it more likely for me to be able to make a big play in a game situation. It's exactly the same in business.

—John Hannah

MAKE ACCOUNTABILITY PART OF YOUR CULTURE BY . . . PUTTING FRONTLINE PEOPLE IN CHARGE OF THE "HOW DO WE DO THIS BETTER?" DISCUSSION

How do you make sustainable improvements in accountability within your organization? Here's an innovative model that drafts frontline employees and gives them a chance to deliver on and defend ideas for doing things better. This delivers ownership and buy-in!

"A Frontline-Driven Process"

Perfecting quality in a sustainable way is always, I have found, a frontline-driven process. It's never a top-down process. So, we're putting our people in charge of the discussion. We're taking them out of the work-flow for a while and putting them on the frontlines,

(Continued)

making a carefully chosen group of 10 or 12 people the key players in identifying some new, leaner processes that will do a better job of delivering value to the customer over time.

We've learned that there has to be shared accountability for a new process to work—and that is very different from siloed accountability! So, one job is getting people out of their silos. In any given group that's working on making a change, two-thirds of the people are not from the area where the change would occur. We don't just want the content expert. We don't just want the person who delivers the service. We want a fresh set of eyes, and that means we want people from outside of the department on the team, too. That gives us diversity of thinking and multiple perspectives on what the customer will actually experience.

People set aside four days. They spend the whole first day out on the floor, observing and measuring exactly what happens on the frontlines from beginning to end and coming up with ideas for making it better for the customer. Then, on days two and three, people are actually simulating the new process they want, in real time. They are empowered to change the process as it's unfolding, right there on the floor. By the fourth day, the new process is in place. But the question remains: Is it delivering on our expectation in a measurable, sustainable way? Is it moving the needle in the right direction over time?

To answer those questions, we have 30-day, 60-day, and 90-day review sessions, where those same people
(Continued)

(Continued)

who revised what was happening on the ground come in and talk to the whole organization about the customer impact and the sustainability of what they've implemented. During those review sessions, everybody gets to know your business. We encourage people from all around the organization to ask tough questions, play devil's advocate, and find out if all the angles have been thought through. We've found that transparency and peer pressure can be wonderful things when it comes to breaking down silos and supporting shared accountability.

—Joan Magruder

MAKE ACCOUNTABILITY PART OF YOUR CULTURE BY . . . ENCOURAGING MEANINGFUL DEBATES

As a general but very reliable rule, people will only assume accountability for initiatives once they feel that they have been listened to. If your organization *does not* do a good job of listening to people—if it does not encourage people to share their insights, concerns, and frustrations in a positive way—then you are going to have a hard time getting them to do the things that will actually support your goals.

Make it part of your organizational culture to talk through the successes *and* the challenges that come your way. Give people permission to contribute, to share problems, and to take part in a fair and an open discussion. Once you do that, you will find them much more likely to assume accountability over time for taking action on the goals you've set out.

Do Your People Feel That They've Been Heard?

We've got to trust people. We've got to hear them out. We've got to be able to get everyone to come in and have a real debate, a real discussion with real frustrations, and then we've got to walk out of the room with everybody being on the same page. Now, we may have had to go through some bloodletting in order to get there, and there may not always be complete consensus on everything that was discussed, but all the viewpoints are explored in that discussion. That way, people can feel that they've been heard; they can walk out of the room and say, "Okay, let's go do it."

—Bill Whitacre

MAKE ACCOUNTABILITY PART OF YOUR CULTURE BY . . . ORGANIZING FOR ACCOUNTABILITY

How do you create and sustain a culture of accountability? By organizing for accountability. That means building a structure that teaches accountability—that organizes for accountability—and then rewards accountability.

Consistent Standards

You focus on the team. All of our results and all of our incentives are evaluated based on team performance,
(Continued)

(Continued)
not on individual performance. So, my incentive com-
pensation metrics as the CEO are the same as the
people who report to me, and theirs are the same as
the people who report to them, and theirs are the same
as the people who report to them. So, it's not a different set of standards. It's very consistent, from the
frontline to the most senior levels of management.
—Steve Lipstein

MAKE ACCOUNTABILITY PART OF YOUR CULTURE BY . . . REVIEWING YOUR STRATEGIC INTENT AND YOUR RIGHT THINGS WITH OTHERS

Over and over again, the Accountability Masters I spoke
with emphasized the importance of committing each team
member's goals and tactics to paper and ensuring that the
team member had the opportunity to review his or her
goals and tactics with another person on a regular basis.

Share the Plan!

Every individual in our firm has what we call a performance development plan, or PDP. Each year, that
person works with his or her counselor to set out the
five or six most important things to accomplish in the
next year. Those goals have to be clearly aligned with
the business unit the person is working in. So, if you
(Continued)

are working in a real estate industry group, we know what that group as a whole is trying to accomplish, and then we look at the individuals within that group and say, "How can you contribute to the success of the real estate group this year? What are the five or six important things you should do to help the unit achieve its goals?" Then, we have a process throughout the next 12 months where there is a progress review.

You need a counselor who leads the discussion and helps you review your progress on your plan, so you can remain accountable to that and see what progress you're actually making. I have a counselor, and so does every single person in the firm.

—Jim Castellano

MAKE ACCOUNTABILITY PART OF YOUR CULTURE BY . . . BEING READY AND WILLING TO BE AN "ACCOUNTABILITY MENTOR"

The instinct of finding someone to be accountable to is, for some of us, an essential part of establishing self-accountability. Not everyone on your team will need this kind of "accountability mentor," but you should constantly be asking yourself who does and be prepared to play that role when it is appropriate.

"I Am Accountable to You!"

Rich DeVos is the owner of our team and the cofounder of the Amway organization. He is 82 years old and for

(Continued)

> *(Continued)*
>
> many years has supported an older evangelist named Anthony Zeoli and has helped to fund his ministry. Every Sunday morning at 9:00, Rich's phone rang at home, and Rich knew who it was. Rich would pick up the phone and say, "Good morning, Anthony," and then Anthony would start telling Rich all the things he had done that week. One morning, Rich said, "Anthony, you know you don't have to call me like this." And Anthony said, "Yes I do, because I am accountable to you—you give the ministry this money, I have to be accountable to you for that." Rich loves to tell that story; the point, I think, is that all of us are accountable to someone.
>
> —Pat Williams

MAKE ACCOUNTABILITY PART OF YOUR CULTURE BY . . . FOCUSING ON VALUES FIRST AND LAWS SECOND

Which would you prefer: for your people to hold themselves accountable for staying out of trouble by following the rules or for them to be accountable for thinking creatively and consistently, taking action on your organization's core values? All of the Accountability Masters I interviewed favored the latter option.

> ### Beyond "Following the Rules"?
>
> Sometimes, organizations send people the message, "We have a lot of rules and a lot of laws here, and you'd
> *(Continued)*

better follow them all." We keep telling people, in other words, "Here are the laws, and if you break the laws, then you are bad." For instance, "If you don't meet X, Y, and Z performance expectations when you interact with a customer, then you are bad." I'm not really fond of that kind of discussion. I'd prefer to talk about principles. I'd prefer to throw the rulebooks out as much as you possibly can and then tell people what the organization's core values are. In this model, you're saying something very different to the team: "Here's how we interact with each other, here's how we interact with a customer, and here's what we want to achieve. Go make that happen." To the degree that it's possible, you want to give people the freedom to take action as they see fit within the broad outlines of those principles and give them the freedom to do what they think is right. Of course, this is a challenge. A lot of people in any organization are going to feel a little uncomfortable with that standard, and there will occasionally be problems you need to sort out. But I think that there is a much bigger upside waiting for your customers and for your business when you give people the authority to navigate in a way that feels comfortable to them.

Ultimately, what you really want people to think about is what they need to do to follow through on the values you've established for your organization. There are probably 30 important meetings going on here at any given time, and I am not going to be in all of those meetings. Many people are operating at

(Continued)

(Continued)
many different levels. If I have made it clear to them exactly where we are headed and exactly what the guiding principles and values of the organization are, then I can feel very confident about what's happening in all those meetings. I can trust that people will very likely make the right decision about the way forward.

—Peter Aceto

MAKE ACCOUNTABILITY PART OF YOUR CULTURE BY . . . MAKING SURE THE TEAM FEELS SUPPORTED

Don't *assume* your people know that you will back them up as they move forward to take action on your strategic intent. Make absolutely *sure* they know! Communication with the team should constantly reinforce this message: "I am delegating responsibility *and* authority to you."

Delegate Responsibility and Authority

If you want people within your organization to hold themselves accountable for something, you have to give them *both* authority and responsibility. A lot of people know they're being held responsible, but they also feel that no one in management is backing them

(Continued)

---

up when they try to fulfill that responsibility, so they don't hold themselves accountable. If they don't feel supported by management, then they're not supported.

—Craig Lovett

MAKE ACCOUNTABILITY PART OF YOUR CULTURE BY . . . INTELLIGENTLY ADJUSTING YOUR EXPECTATIONS

Sometimes, the team will uncover an important new piece of information or propose a paradigm-shifting new idea that justifies revising the expectations that you and the team have set. Be open to these moments. Honor your team's creativity by showing enough flexibility to change the target when circumstances warrant.

"See Where the Path Leads"

Be aware that there will be times when your team identifies a major crossroads for you that you hadn't noticed. A new event or a new piece of information can lead you in a completely different direction, a direction that is quite beyond the boundaries of the expectations you've set up. You don't want to follow every new path, of course, but you don't want to reject that new path instantly, either. Strike a balance. Have reasonable expectations, and if an event happens that leads your team in a

(Continued)

(*Continued*)
promising new direction, have some fun, see where the path leads, and keep an open mind. Don't refuse to explore the path just because it isn't part of your grand plan.

—Clem Sunter

MAKE ACCOUNTABILITY PART OF YOUR CULTURE BY . . . DEMONSTRATING YOUR OWN COMMITMENT TO FOCUS ON THE RIGHT THINGS

In centuries past, the architect who had designed an arch for a town would demonstrate his accountability for his own work by being the first person to stand beneath the arch when the construction supports were removed. Make no mistake! Your team is looking for the same level of accountability from you, and they will begin by looking at the choices you make about your own right things.

Accountability for Doing the Right Things Flows from the Top Down

Leaders *must* focus on the right things—because if the CEO is focusing on the wrong things, that is not going to help in getting the organization as a whole up to
(*Continued*)

speed. The people who work for that CEO are inevitably going to spend their time focusing on what the CEO is focusing on. Like it or not, we set the tone.

—Gerry Czarnecki

The conversation about how to build an accountable organization is, of course, an ongoing one. Please join it by visiting www.SamSilverstein.com.

Conclusion:
The Accountability Movement

There came a moment early on in the process of developing this book when I realized that each and every one of the Highly Accountable People I was interviewing was a member of a special group.

Each of these successful individuals had a powerful shared cause with the other achievers I was interviewing: Each was on a mission to recruit new accountable people by helping them to recognize and expand their own Accountability Zones. Each of these Accountability Masters was saying, "There are accountable people, and there is everyone else. Join us!"

This "accountability cause" transcended even their own personal or professional intentions. In fact, this cause supported everything they did. It enriched every alliance they made, supported every project they undertook, and invigorated every goal. It transformed their very sense of self. They all loved talking about people they had inspired to reclaim long-dormant Accountability Zones.

Each of these people, I realized, was an active participant in what amounted to a global movement: the movement to build accountability into families, organizations, and nations, one person at a time. They each supported that movement by expanding their own Accountability Zone and by spreading the word about the power of the Five Accountabilities to others.

My challenge to you as we close is simple: Join our movement.

Become a highly accountable person. Implement the Five Accountabilities in your own life, and share the message with others. Then, share your stories about building a culture of accountability within your own family, in the workplace, and in the larger world.

If you're willing to become part of our movement—and by this point, I hope you are—you can begin the job of building a more accountable world by building a more accountable you. That means practicing and implementing what you've learned here about right things, new space, managing the process, establishing expectations, and contributing to relationships. It means reaching the point in your life where you can say, *"No More Excuses!* I'm not going to make excuses, and I'm not going to buy excuses, and I want the world to know that."

It also means spreading the word about accountability by your own consistent example and by direct invitation. No matter what you may have been through in your life, you can always expand your own Accountability Zone, and you can inspire others to do the same. You can practice the Five Accountabilities in your own life, and you can talk about the accountabilities regularly with the people you meet. You can also share this book. Most of the people I interviewed about the Five Accountabilities were eager to see the finished book so that they could share it with other people in their life; it's likely that you, too, know someone who would benefit by reading about these principles.

Spread the word. Always begin with yourself. If you wish to change the culture of your family, your department, or the larger world, you will find, as I have, that a Culture of Accountability always begins with personal choices and that accountable relationships always involve individuals, not organizations.

Please share your experiences and your own insights on accountability with me by visiting www.SamSilverstein. com.

I look forward to hearing from you! Remember: *Accountability is not a consequence . . . accountability is your competitive advantage!*

THE FOLLOWING CHAPTER IS AN EXCERPT FROM

NON-NEGOTIABLE

BY SAM SILVERSTEIN

Do you ever find yourself questioning what you believe around issues that impact your life and business? Do you ever feel lost in your decisions? Are you ever frustrated in your lack of ability to take your life or business exactly where you know you want to go?

Non-Negotiable *is about understanding what you believe, what you can control, what your mission is, and ultimately taking your convictions to the level of Non-Negotiable.*

1

How I Met Pat Hickman

A couple of years back, I had just finished speaking to a leadership group in Amarillo, Texas when I found myself upstaged.

That doesn't happen very often at events where I am the main speaker, and when it does I want to find out why it happens—so I can raise my game.

My topic that day had been accountability, my favorite subject. It's so much so that I wrote a book, *No More Excuses*, which is really my life's message. So when I speak, I am passionate, convinced, and committed to the accountability strategies I believe transform lives and organizations.

As I walked away from the podium that day in Amarillo, the crowd applauded enthusiastically. That's a good sign, I thought to myself, because these were people I wanted to do business with. Sharon Miner—a community leader in Amarillo who I later asked to come on board and become my director of operations—had organized this opportunity, and that was the whole reason I was here: to create new business ventures.

When I took my seat, though, another man strode forward, and when he stepped onto the stage, something happened in that room. The moment he took his position in front of the microphone, the whole ambience changed.

His name, he said, was J. Pat Hickman, and he was the CEO of Happy State Bank. Just hearing the unlikely name of his outfit, Happy State Bank, told me something was going to be different.

A PRESENCE AS BIG AS TEXAS

Pat wore a big pair of cowboy boots. In fact, I remember thinking that absolutely everything about him was big. He filled every single inch of that room, not just because he's a tall man, but because of his large presence and his sense of a serious personal goal. From the very first words he spoke, everyone in that room, including me, could sense that he was here for a reason. A big reason. A reason you wanted to know more about.

Within seconds, Pat had won over everyone, and I do mean everyone, who was in that room. Sharon saw it. I saw it.

As a professional speaker myself—and a past president of the National Speakers Association (NSA®)—I've been watching speakers long enough to know when someone has the audience on his or her side. This audience was definitely on Pat's side, but that wasn't all that had happened. In just a few minutes, he had them totally committed to his agenda. I remember looking around the room of standing, cheering people, and thinking that every single one of these people looked ready to open an account at Happy State Bank, apply to work there, or both! It was as though everything had become possible, for Pat and for everybody else, in just a matter of minutes.

> Accountability is my favorite subject—so much so that I wrote a book, *No More Excuses*, which is really my life's message. So when I speak, I am passionate, convinced, and committed to the accountability strategies I believe transform lives and organizations.

That flat-out astonished me. Who was this guy? Was he for real? How in the world had he done that? What were we all cheering for?

Something about what Pat Hickman had done was jaw-dropping alright, but I couldn't quite figure out what it was. I remember thinking at the time that he was either the genuine article, of a kind I had never encountered...or maybe, just maybe, the greatest con man west of the Mississippi.

PAT HAD ANSWERS

It's a little bit embarrassing to me now to own up that I wasn't quite sure which of those people I was looking at on the first day I encountered Pat Hickman. I do know I felt equal parts astonishment and skepticism as I watched Pat speak that day. Maybe I leaned more toward the skepticism. Maybe that's just how I am with new people who seem to have all the big answers to all the big questions. Maybe, at times, I wasn't sure anyone had answers to *any* of the big questions. And maybe I was sure no one could really be as "on"—at least not all the time—as Pat seemed to be during that speech. So yes, I suppose I was happy to assume that this guy was just a little too good to be true.

As it turned out, I was wrong about that. Very wrong.

Pat spent a lot of time that day talking about the mission of his organization: "Work hard, have fun, make money, while providing outstanding customer service and honoring the Golden Rule."

Something about the way he said that made me sit up and take notice.

Pat's words rushed over me like a waterfall during that speech. I remember that he also talked a lot about his employees. He told us where Happy State Bank's unique name came from, what its customer service standards were, and how the people who worked at the bank did their best to live up to that name and those standards. He shared how his people flat-out loved working at that bank, and how he loved working there, too. He was not ashamed to discuss his personal faith in Jesus Christ with anyone, and how that was the success of his bank. Take the time right now to reread his foreword and you'll see exactly what I mean. I especially remember him talking about his "absolutes"—the standards, the non-negotiables—he and his bank set in place that were not open to debate.

He talked about all of that—his belief system, his bank's mission, their non-negotiables—in a straightforward, compelling way. He talked about it all in much greater depth in my subsequent interviews with him—interviews I will share with you as this story unfolds. The main thing you need to know now, though, is what I took away on that very first day. It was a curiosity combined with a sense of skepticism I have already shared with you, the sense that this man was not, could not possibly be, for real.

I couldn't get it off my mind. How could a business leader in any industry, much less the banking industry, spend 20 minutes talking about the Golden Rule—and inspire a room full of skeptical people? What made him so special? Why him?

There had to be a catch somewhere.

The worst part was that I was a little afraid I had fallen under Pat's spell. Every once in a while, I caught myself thinking that I, too, wanted to work with this guy.

Why?

Was I growing soft?

Now I wanted to figure out who this man really was. During a break, I introduced myself to Pat and made a little small talk. I didn't get much time to size him up. I had to head off to another meeting Sharon had scheduled, so I made a mental note to research Pat and his bank after I made it back home to St. Louis. I wanted to call him.

I promised myself, though: There will be no giving in to the notion about *me* jumping on his bandwagon. I already had a bandwagon—accountability. Pat and his happy bank were a prospective client at that point. An interesting prospect. A prospect I was a little curious about. But nothing more. Or so I told myself as I left the hall.

Surprisingly, though, Pat and I were to meet much

sooner than I expected.

HE WAS A MAN WITH A PURPOSE

Sharon had set up a luncheon the following day inviting leaders from the community to come hear about the accountability movement I steer. There were 15 people present including Pat Hickman.

I greeted Pat and cautiously talked with him before we sat down to our round table session. I kept waiting for some kind of sign that he was faking it. It never came. Everything still seemed possible. He still was a man with a purpose.

What was this guy's game? I still hadn't figured him out.

HE READ MY BOOK

A month later, I was preparing to go back to Amarillo. I was scheduled to meet the general manager of a local network television affiliate station, the president of the Amarillo-Canyon business incubator, and even the mayor of Amarillo. (Canyon is a nearby town that's home to West Texas A&M University and an integral partner in the success of the Panhandle community.)

A thought passed through my mind: *As long as I'm in Amarillo....*

I asked Sharon whether, on this visit, we could stop by Happy State Bank and visit Pat Hickman.

Pat was still a prospect, I told myself. Just a prospect. Nothing more. Yet somehow, this was the meeting I was most looking forward to.

Sharon and I showed up for the meeting with Pat a

few minutes early. He came out of his office to greet us and showed us in personally. His personality and charisma were just as big as I remembered. Within seconds, it somehow felt like we had been friends for a very long time.

As we settled in, Pat pointed to a copy of my book on accountability, *No More Excuses*, which was displayed prominently on his desk.

Pat said, "Your book has been on my desk longer than any other book. It's not because I haven't read it. It's because I've been showing it to everyone who walks in the room!"

We chatted for a while. I learned more about Pat and his bank. Then all of a sudden the conversation changed direction. Pat stood up from the sitting area, went to his desk, and printed off four sheets of paper. He handed them to me and said, "I want you to know what we believe. This is our unofficial values document. It's our list of 'absolutes.' It goes much deeper than what you see on these pages, though."

I read that list of values over several times and felt something shifting inside of me. It was as if he had just handed me 20 diamonds. It was their list of 20 absolutes. Their list of 20 values they did not deviate on. It was *No More Excuses* in action!

I asked Pat whether the commitments were listed in their order of importance. I guess maybe I was looking for a loophole. He shook his head, "No."

"They're all important," he said. "No one value on the list is more or less important than any other. This is how we do business."

Those 20 diamonds—those 20 absolutes—inspired

this book and the title. I saw that list as Happy State Bank's non-negotiables—and I believe everyone and every organization needs their own non-negotiables.

Each and every one of Happy State Bank's Non-Negotiable Core Values™ was totally consistent with the bank's mission: *Work hard, have fun, make money, while providing outstanding customer service and honoring the Golden Rule.*

Not only that, each and every one of Happy State Bank's Non-Negotiable Core Values was totally consistent with Pat's personal belief system.

HE WANTED ME TO WRITE THEIR HAPPY STORY

Without even meaning to, I had opened the door to the secret vault that held what made both Pat and the bank tick—and clearly demonstrate my message of accountability. Just by interacting with him, I could tell that Pat had fully committed to each of these non-negotiables personally—even though he called them by a different name.

While I felt honored that he would share his list of core values with me, I was still skeptical for some reason. I still wondered if anyone could really be as authentic as Pat seemed to be, and I questioned if anyone could actually consistently stick to these principles. There are lots of companies with words on a piece of paper.

Fine. This was what Pat was willing to commit to. I could accept the idea that this was how he personally did business—or wanted to. Did that mean every single person in the organization really bought in to all 20 of these values? The entire Happy State Bank culture was built around them? Was that even possible? Somehow, this still wasn't making sense to me.

TIME TO WRITE *NON-NEGOTIABLE*

Just as that thought flashed across my mind, though, Pat said, "This may sound like a crazy question, Sam, but I am going to ask it anyway. I have had several people ask to write a book about our bank, but it's never felt right. Is there any chance *you* might be interested in writing that book?"

I hadn't expected that one.

Pat went on: "People are always telling me there should be a book that tells our story, but I never have found the right person. I think it ought to be you."

Pat and I talked the idea over, and before I left the room I agreed to give the matter some thought and get back to him. I told him I was interested, and that I would let him know my decision once I made it back to my office in St. Louis.

But on my way out of Amarillo, I questioned the fit. I thought it all over, and I found lots more reasons *not* to go forward with the book project than reasons to write it.

How much did I really know about this guy? All in all, I had only spent a couple of hours with him. What made this the right project for me? When had I ever written about another person or another business as the sole topic of a book? What profit could I make on such a deal? How would that profit compare to something else I might be doing with my time? I admit it. I was looking at the dollars first.

When I got back to St. Louis, I put together an

elaborate proposal based on a similar project an author friend of mine had completed for a big company. It was a substantial deal. It covered all sorts of costs, marketing fees, and production expenses. When we had our next meeting and I presented the proposal to Pat. There was an obvious pause.

Pat said, "There is no way I can go to my board with a six-figure proposal." It just didn't work for Pat. Pat's a banker, not a publisher. He didn't want to proceed. We decided to let things lie.

Several weeks passed and I called Sharon. She said, "Sam, I've been thinking about that proposal."

I said, "I have too." I went over all my misgivings with her. I value her opinion and I needed it. We talked about how Pat didn't want to proceed with our proposal. I finally said to Sharon, "He just doesn't get the book business I guess."

That was just an excuse. In fact, this wasn't about Pat at all at this point. I was the one who wasn't getting it. As I told Sharon that I was about to tell Pat I didn't think the book project was a good fit, my explanation ended with the rhetorical musing, "Why me?"

There was a long silence.

Eventually I had to check to see whether or not Sharon was still on the line. She was.

"I'll tell you why it should be you, Sam," she said. "I watched you when Pat talked at the leadership event in Amarillo. I watched you at the round table. And I watched you during the meeting we had with Pat at the bank. Something about you changes when Pat's in the room. You think about what is possible in a different way. You have a different way of looking at your own purpose. He's got an important story to tell. And you need to hear it, too. I am telling you, Sam, if you walk away from this project, you will regret it. And if you ask me, you were born to do this book."

Now the silence was on my end of the line. I knew Sharon was right. I knew, in my heart, that I was meant to tell this story. It was an expansion of teaching accountability. It was an expansion of *No More Excuses*.

"Pat has spoken on several occasions of providence in his life. If providence is present in Pat's life, and if it brought the two of us together, then it must be present in my life, too," I admitted. Not only did I say that, but also I felt it in my heart! A few months earlier I might have struggled to say that, but the events happening in my life were affecting me, and in a good way. The door was open and I needed to walk through it. I just needed to say, "Yes."

"You're right, Sharon," I said. "I gotta run. Bye."

I had practically hung up on Sharon, but now it was clear as day what I needed to do and I didn't want to waste a minute. I called Pat and asked him, "Are you still interested in me writing that book?"

He responded, "Yes I am."

"Well, we are going to find a way to do this. Forget the agreement. Forget the cost. I'll write the book. We'll figure out who will publish it and how all the pieces go together as we proceed." I moved forward at that moment with great calmness, because inside I recognized what I really believed and I knew this was what I was supposed to do. Period!

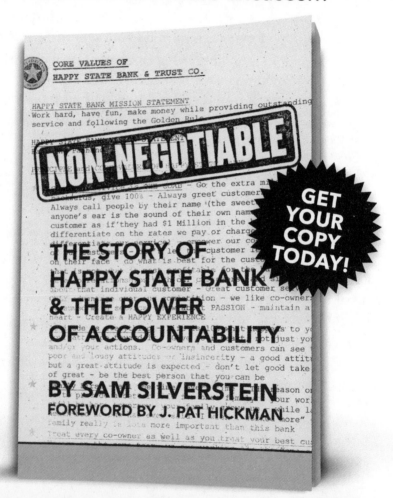

INDEX

Index

Index

AUTHOR BIOGRAPHY

Sam Silverstein is founder and CEO of Sam Silverstein Enterprises, Inc., an accountability think tank dedicated to helping companies create an organizational culture that prioritizes and inspires accountability. Based on helping organizations develop what they believe in, clarify their mission, and understand what is in their control, Sam works to make this a more accountable world. Mr. Silverstein is the author of several books including *Non-Negotiable* and *Making Accountable Choices*. He is a highly sought-after speaker, having worked with teams of companies, government agencies, and organizations both big and small, including Kraft Foods, Pfizer, United States Air Force, and United Way. He is a former president of the National Speakers Association.

For more information on having Sam Silverstein speak at your event, or work with your organization, please contact us at info@samsilverstein.com.